はしがき

　私達は沢山の「商品」[*]に囲まれ、それらを購入し、食べたり使ったりして日々生活しています。商品を作り、販売するのは「企業」です。企業は私達から収入を得て、必要な支出を行い、また次の新しい商品を開発し、発展しようと努力します。企業が発展して行くには、独自の「価値」を持つ商品が必要です。選ばれて、買ってもらうための「魅力」です。値の一つです。価格以外の価値が乏しい「特徴がない商品」の場合　　　　　　　　　　　　　　　に陥ります。これは企業にとっては恐怖の負のスパイラルです。

（*）商品：モノとしての製品と形のないサービスの両

　このテキストでは正反対の、「独自の価値を創った商品」「その商品を創った企業と経営」を皆さんに理解していただくのが主な目的です。なぜなら、それが真に優れたビジネスであり、皆さんが将来の目標にすべきだからです。日本の商品は世界で高く評価されていますが、主な理由は「質が良い」、「不良品がなく、故障しない」「良く考えられた機能がある」などの価値です。簡単に言えば安心して買える商品だからです。「安いから」が理由の商品は極めて少ないのです。実は日本企業も最初からそのような商品を作れたわけではありません。先人達が大変な苦労を重ねながら、「消費者が喜んで買う商品とは何か」を追求した結果に優れた技術が組み合わさって、続々と独自価値の高い商品が生まれました。それこそが、日本が経済成長を遂げ世界から信頼されてきた最大の理由です。

　このテキストが類書と異なるのは、商品の企画・開発を中心に企業とその経営を学んでいただく点です。本書での紹介を快く受けていただいた企業は超大企業から中小企業まで、業種も多種多様ですが「優れた商品」を独自に開発し、成功しているという一点で共通しています。執筆するに当たり、すべての企業に足を運び直接社員の方々にインタビューさせていただきました。特に開発を担当される方にお話を伺う機会を持てたことは喜びです。深く理解していただくために、会社の歴史や風土なども紹介しますが「なぜこの会社はこのような素晴らしい商品を創れたのか」「どのように考え、どのような経緯や方法で開発できたのか」が必ず描かれています。中には「幸運だった」と語る方もおられましたが、世の中の流れを読み、新たなニーズを探り商品化したのであり決して運などではありません。

　お忙しい中を取材や資料のご提供にご協力いただいた各社の皆様には心からの謝意を表します。また、英訳、リスニングと設問の作成をいただいた先生方、本書の企画から取材・編集・校正に至るまで尽力いただいた松柏社の永野啓子さん、多くの方々の努力で本書は完成することができました。誠にありがとうございます。

神田　範明

CONTENTS

Morinaga
— Refuel your body in 10 seconds

INTRODUCTION 「in ゼリー」は、1994 年の発売以降変化し続ける顧客の志向にいかに対応し、巨大ヒット商品に成長して維持・拡大を続けているのだろうか？

Step 1 ▶▶▶ Vocabulary Buildup

Match the words and phrases below with the correct meanings in Japanese.

1.	embark on **1**	～で決まる
2.	beverage **1**	妨げる
3.	critical **2**	～の希望に合わせて
4.	nutrition **2**	栄養
5.	hinder **2**	～を主演にした
6.	cumbersome **3**	～としてほめる (as)
7.	tout **5**	～に乗り出す
8.	skyrocket **5**	爆発的に伸びる
9.	featuring **5**	飲み物
10.	cater to **6**	重要な
11.	adapt **7**	～に適応する
12.	hinge on **7**	運びづらい

Reading

Audio 1-02

1 More than two decades ago, Morinaga & Co., Ltd., a maker of well-known chocolates, snacks, ice cream, and other treats, embarked on developing a new beverage for athletes. The hope was that it would eventually also have a broader consumer appeal.

5

2 The first idea was a liquid drink, but athletes complained that it sat too heavily in their stomachs when playing sports. One professional athlete provided a critical piece of advice. The suggestion was for a drink that provides nutrition but is easy to consume. Also, it should be

10 filling, but not so much that it hinders sports activities immediately after drinking.

3 Morinaga turned to a liquid jelly the company had sold earlier in its history. This one had been packaged in a glass

15 bottle, but this would be too heavy and cumbersome for athletes, as well as for the general consumers the company was hoping to also target. This time, Morinaga decided to use a

20 more lightweight can instead. However, this design looked too similar to other sports drinks. The solution was to put the drink into an aluminum pouch with a straw, also called a spout pouch.

「飲むゼリー」

4 Now Morinaga had both the right ingredients and the right container, and

25 *in Jelly* was launched in 1994. The product would go on to become a huge hit because it developed a mass appeal beyond the narrow market of athletes to busy people in general.

5 Initially, *in Jelly* was sold in sporting goods stores and gyms, but then a purchaser from a major convenience store

30 chain saw it. He arranged with Morinaga to sell *in Jelly* on a trial basis in convenience stores. Another step toward greater popularity was an advertising campaign. Targeting a wider

consumer audience, the ads presented *in Jelly* as a quick and healthy substitute for a traditional breakfast and touted it as a morning meal you can 35 down in 10 seconds. Sales then skyrocketed. Later commercials featuring a famous Japanese actor reshaped *in Jelly's* image as more than just a breakfast option and claimed that a 10-second charge would keep a person energized and active for a long 40 while.

6 There has always been demand for this kind of simple product among busy people, but it has grown recently as more Japanese women enter the workforce and workers in general seek greater time efficiency as 45 working lifestyles change. A parallel development is a widespread increase in health awareness and demand for meals with good nutritional balance. These two factors have likely driven *in Jelly's* recent sales growth. To better cater to these customers, Morinaga 50 has expanded *in Jelly's* lineup, with varieties for energy, vitamins, minerals, protein, and more.

7 A product does not become a hit without a reason, and if it does, sustained growth requires considerable effort. Product developers must constantly innovate 55 and adapt. Furthermore, success hinges on being customer-focused, while the process must be revalidated every step of the way. Morinaga has done this for the past 25 years, creating a niche market and a product with sustained popularity. You have to tip 60 your cap to Morinaga.

● l. 1：& Co., Ltd. (= and Company Limited) 株式会社 ● l. 2：treat おいしいお菓子、ごちそう ● l. 10：filling 満腹感を与える ● l. 23：spout pouch キャップ付パウチ：軽量、低価格、環境にやさしい ● l. 24：ingredient 成分 ● l. 27：in general 一般の ● l. 29：purchaser バイヤー、購買者 ● l. 33：ads 広告 ● l. 44：workforce 労働力 ● l. 58：revalidate 正しいか再確認する ● l. 59：niche market すきま市場：他社が進出していない未開拓市場 ● ll. 60-61：tip your cap 敬意をしめす：帽子を少し脱いで、傾けて会釈する様から

Step 2 ▶▶▶ Comprehension Questions

After reading the passage, choose either True (T), False (F), or "No information available in the passage"(?) for the statements below.

1. Morinaga first targeted *in Jelly* at the busy people working for the companies.

(　　)

2. Aluminum (pouch) containers cost higher than glass ones. (　　)

3. Sales skyrocketed after the TV commercial ads reshaped the product's image.

(　　)

4. Advertising campaign is one of the factors contributing to the product success. (　　)

5. Morinaga has been making considerable efforts for the past quarter of the century. (　　)

Step 3 ▶▶▶ One More Episode

🔊 Audio 1-03

Listen and fill in the blanks.

Morinaga was founded in (1)_____ by Morinaga Taichiro after studying in (2)_____. There, he had learned how to make Western confectioneries, and these were the company's first products, such as caramel. In the (3)_____, the company (4)_____ the first integrated production facility in Japan to make chocolate from cocoa beans. Morinaga may be (5)_____ known for its snacks, but did you know that during World War II the company succeeded in producing penicillin in Japan? (6)_____ the technology and knowledge attained (7)_____ many years in business, Morinaga continues to make products that enrich our diets and promote health.

森永製菓本社 (東京都)

● **penicillin** ペニシリン：結核の特効薬

Step 4 ▶▶▶ Interaction

Make pairs and ask each other questions given below.

1. What is your favorite breakfast menu and why?
2. What recent TV commercial do you like best and why?

Step 5 ▶▶▶ Summary & Presentation

Q 1. Summarize the passage by using the following keywords.

athlete   *in Jelly*   busy people   spout pouch

breakfast   energize   lifestyle   niche market

Q 2. **Make a presentation** of the summary made above.

Hibiya Kadan  HIBIYA-KADAN
—— Flowers making up various scenes

結婚式では定番の、花にまつわるあることは同社の提案で始まったもの。「花のカタログ」販売の
工夫と苦心。そして、あるビジネス進出までのプロセスとは？

Step 1 ▶▶▶ Vocabulary Buildup

Match the words and phrases below with the correct meanings in Japanese.

1. lush **1** ● ● 着手する
2. in charge of ~ **2** ● ● 必須な
3. essential **2** ● ● （…に）帰する
4. establish **3** ● ● （…を）実行する
5. roll out **4** ● ● 設立する
6. launch **5** ● ● （…を）受け入れる
7. provide with **6** ● ● （新商品を）発表する
8. embrace **6** ● ● （…を）満たす
9. implement **6** ● ● ～担当の
10. attribute to ~ **7** ● ● 青々とした
11. fulfill **7** ● ● （…を）提供する

Reading

📶 **Audio 1-04**

1 Hibiya Park is an urban oasis covering 160,000 m^2 in Tokyo's Hibiya district, near the Imperial Palace. Did you know there is a fine flower shop at the central entrance of this lush green park? It belongs to Hibiya Kadan, a company that adopted its current name when it opened this 5 store.

創業当時（右端の法被を着ている方が創業者）

2 The founder ran a successful gardening business in the Horikiri area of Katsushika, eastern Tokyo. Thanks to excellent work and good connections, the company was put in 10 charge of the Imperial Hotel gardens. Then, it further expanded business by providing flowers for hotel guestrooms and party venues upon request. It was Hibiya Kadan that introduced Japan to the hitherto unknown custom of the wedding bouquet, as well as the idea of the groom and bride presenting their parents a gift of flowers. Today, this act is an essential part of Japanese weddings for expressing gratitude to family.

15

店舗の外観と内観（1960年代）

3 In 1950, the company received a 20 request from Tokyo's governor to open a flower shop in Hibiya Park, a place of rest and recreation for Tokyoites. The idea was an extension of the company's philosophy. Starting 25 with Hibiya, by around the 1980s the company had branches in major cities across Japan, had provided flowers for historical moments such as the Tsukuba Expo and Expo '90, and had built a global flower procurement network while establishing a firm position as a nationwide 30 chain selling sophisticated flowers.

大阪花博（1990年）

4 The company rolled out a series of new flower services. Although selling flowers via catalogs is ordinary today, the business of delivering fresh flowers was a challenge. How could they be transported while staying fresh? Hibiya Kadan worked out a method by providing detailed instructions to keep arranged flowers appearing exactly like their photographs, developing an original delivery box, and adding a window so couriers can see the contents.

5 In 1994, Hibiya Kadan launched an e-commerce business before it was even a word. It was the personal computer boom, and customers could order flowers with these new devices. The company then commenced full-scale online sales in 2001, which was quicker than the competition in flowers and other industries.

通販サイト

Then, in 2004, the company expanded into the business

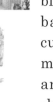

of personal funeral services. Before, Hibiya Kadan had only arranged and delivered flower displays for funerals, but decided to take it a step further by organizing entire funerals.

6 Thus, Hibiya Kadan's products and services have blossomed because they are consistently created based on customer needs and the company's cumulative experience. Product planners conduct market surveys and deduce needs from customers and store clerks. The company's spirit embraces challenge, while employees are given wide discretion. This combination is conducive to implementing new services. When a customer provided feedback that the departed's photograph looked dark in a black picture frame, the company produced a brightly colored one. And when another said they wanted to keep memories of this final event with the deceased person, Hibiya Kadan sent a photographer to make a memorial album covering the entire funeral.

7 There is always a reason why a company grows large. In Hibiya Kadan's case, the success is attributable to close familiarity with what their customers do and an unlimited earnestness to fulfill their requests.

Notes

● l. 2 : district 地区 ● ll. 7-8 : run a business 商売を営む ● l. 14 : hitherto これまで ● l. 27 : branch 支店 ● l. 30 : firm 企業 ● l. 31 : sophisticated 洗練された ● l. 33 : via 経由（して） ● l. 37 : courier 宅配便 ● l. 39 : before it was even a word （業界でこの用語が）使われる前から ● l. 45 : funeral 葬式、葬儀 ● l. 51 : base on …に基づいて ● l. 52 : cumulative 累計 ● l. 52 : conduct 実施する ● l. 55 : discretion 裁量 ● l. 56 : conducive 助長する ● l. 57 : departed 故人、死者 ● ll. 60-61 : deceased person 故人 ● l. 64 : attributable to …に起因する

Step 2 ▶▶▶ Comprehension Questions

After reading the passage, choose either True (T), False (F), or "No information available in the passage"(?) for the statements below.

1. The company adopted its current name when it opened the store at the central entrance of the Hibiya Park. ( )

2. Hibiya Kadan originated the idea of giving flowers to the parents in wedding ceremonies. ( )

3. Transporting the fresh flowers was not challenging. ( )

4. Hibiya Kadan was one of the quickest companies in starting full-scale online sales. ( )

5. According to the needs of customers, Hibiya Kadan organized various services. ( )

Step 3 ▶▶▶ One More Episode

🔊 Audio 1-05

Listen and fill in the blanks.

The company has ⁽¹⁾ _____ types of stores. In addition to Hibiya Kadan, which focuses on gifts at hotels and department stores, there is Hibiya Kadan-Style targeting consumers wanting casual gifts or flowers to enjoy at home, ⁽²⁾ _____ Wonder Flower, which provides reasonably priced flowers as materials ⁽³⁾ ____ original arrangements at home.

Customers choose the option that ⁽⁴⁾ _____ their lifestyle or setting. ⁽⁵⁾ _____ companies find it difficult to match this level of meticulous service. Another popular service, Hananohi, allows customers to ⁽⁶⁾ _____ flowers at the store for a flat monthly rate so they ⁽⁷⁾ _____ enjoy them routinely, rather than only for special occasions.

● **meticulous** 細部まで行き届いた ● **a flat monthly rate** 月極め料金で ● **routinely** 定期的に

step 4 ▶▶▶ Interaction

Make pairs and ask each other questions given below.

1. What was the best birthday present you ever received in your life and why was it so special?
2. What online services have you used before and why?

step 5 ▶▶▶ Summary & Presentation

Q 1. Summarize the passage by using the following keywords.

Imperial Hotel   expand   flower service   online

funeral   customer needs   survey   success

_____
_____
_____
_____
_____
_____
_____

Q 2. **Make a presentation** of the summary made above.

Lesson

3

Hoyu
— Live colorfully by dyeing your hair yourself

hoyu
COLOR YOUR HEART

📢 ヘアカラーという専門的な分野に特化し、新規の商品開発と商品の改良を続け、トップメーカー
INTRODUCTION の地位を築いた同社のバックボーンとは？

step 1 ▶▶▶ Vocabulary Buildup

Match the words and phrases below with the correct meanings in Japanese.

1. gray hair **1** ● ● 手頃な
2. remedy **2** ● ● 成分
3. build a reputation **2** ● ● 欠点、欠陥
4. ingredient **2** ● ● 溶かす
5. affordable **2** ● ● 役を演じる、役割を担う
6. dissolve **3** ● ● 適切な、ふさわしい
7. dominant **3** ● ● 個性、特性
8. play a role for **3** ● ● 支配的な、主要な
9. individuality **4** ● ● （人を精神的に）高揚させる
10. shortcoming **5** ● ● よく構成された、構造化された
11. suitable **5** ● ● 〜を支える、〜を大切にする
12. well-structured **5** ● ● 治療、矯正法
13. prioritize **6** ● ● それまでは、
14. speak to **6** ● ● 白髪
15. uplift **6** ● ● 名声を築き上げる
16. meanwhile **6** ● ● 〜に専念する
17. concentrate on **7** ● ● 〜を優先させる

Reading

🔊 **Audio 1-06**

1 When a woman walks down the street with beautifully dyed hair, she looks more youthful. Men who dye their hair are not uncommon, either. Some have it done at a beauty salon, while many color it at home. Nagoya-based Hoyu is a top Japanese maker of hair dye known for brands like *Bigen* for gray hair and *Beautylabo* for dark.

創業者 水野増次郎氏

2 Hoyu began in 1905 as Mizuno Kankudo（水野甘苦堂）, founded by Mizuno Masujiro as a producer and distributor of home remedies. When he was only 12, he built a reputation selling for Nagoya pharmaceutical distributors, then went independent at age 27. At a relative's suggestion, he turned his attention to hair dye, a new product at that time, and began researching on his own. After obtaining the active ingredient, he started selling the company's first hair dye, *Niwakarasu*（二羽からす）, then trademarked it in

1913. Another hair dye, *Genroku*（元禄）, came out in 1921. It became a big hit that appealed to people for many reasons: quality, the innovative formula that only took 30 minutes to dye (when six hours was standard),

元禄の大行燈

the affordable price, and a unique promotional approach of ringing a bell while distributing flyers at parades of giant paper lanterns. *Genroku* remained a hot-selling item for over 70 years.

3 *Bigen*, released in 1957, marked a further breakthrough. The name is a Japanese blended word of "beauty" and "Genroku." While applying *Genroku* involved heating, cooling, and blending three concoctions before dyeing, this successor comprised a single powdered ingredient to dissolve in water. The founder's son, Mizuno Kinpei, established a dominant

share in the market with this excellent product. Now it comes in many more colors and varieties, including a ₃₅ cream and a bubbly version in a pump dispenser. Dye for gray hair accounts for just under 90% of hair color product sales in Japan's market, while that for dark makes up slightly more than 10%. Both *Genroku* and *Bigen* have played important roles in dyeing gray hair in ₄₀ Japan.

4 The lineup also includes easy-to-use *Beautylabo* to give dark hair a beautiful shiny color with fun, *Beauteen* to express one's individuality, and *Men's Bigen* for men with gray hair. Hoyu also sells many ₄₅ professional products to beauty salons. In addition, the company sells many products to hair stylists and other professionals in an overseas market spanning some 70 countries.

5 To develop new series, Hoyu uses group interviews and social media to study lifestyles, attitudes, and wants. To improve on existing products, the company investigates them for ₅₀ dissatisfaction and shortcomings, then matches suitable technology from its lab for product planning. In either case, planning involves matching market needs with Hoyu's resources. It's a well-structured process that involves conducting large questionnaire surveys as ₅₅ needed for thornier problems.

6 The Hoyu concept of "Color Your Heart" is about prioritizing products that speak to sensitivities and wants to make customers, especially women, feel beautiful and uplifted by dyeing their hair. The company culture, meanwhile, is about being "stable and positive." It may sound simple, but implementation ₆₀ is not.

7 Hoyu carefully selects managerial resources to concentrate on the specialist field of hair color, while being stable and positive has been the backbone behind the company's position as a top manufacturer. Leveraging these strengths should lead to even greater things in the future. ₆₅

● l. 1 : dyed hair 染めた髪 ● l. 3 : color 〜に染める ● l. 8 : distributor 代理店、販売業者 ● l. 10 : pharmaceutical 調剤（学）の ● l. 15 : active ingredient 有効成分 ● l. 17 : trademark 登録商標にする ● l. 26 : flyer チラシ、小冊子：宣伝・広告のために人々に配布する印刷物 ● l. 29 : blended word 混成語 ● l. 31 : concoction 調合薬 ● l. 56 : thornier problem より難しい問題 ● l. 62 : managerial resources 経営資源 ● l. 63 : backbone 根幹 ● l. 64 : leverage 投入する、投資する、〜をテコにする

Step 2 ▶▶▶ Comprehension Questions

After reading the passage, choose either True (T), False (F), or "No information available in the passage"(?) for the statements below.

1. Hoyu is a top Japanese maker of hair dye for women. ( )

2. Mizuno Masujiro was only 12 when he went independent from a Nagoya pharmaceutical distributor. ( )

3. Recently, Hoyu's sales increased owing to a pump dispenser. ( )

4. By conducting various surveys, Hoyu continues to match the customer needs. ( )

5. To be stable and positive is the most important thing for Hoyu's future. ( )

Step 3 ▶▶▶ One More Episode

🔊 **Audio 1-07**

Listen and fill in the blanks.

ホーユー本社（愛知県名古屋市）

The company's name, Hoyu, is a Japanese word (1) _____ "friend" or "companion." The idea is about (2) _____ challenges hand-in-hand with a friend and (3) _____ friendly relations with all fans and business partners. Hoyu's founder (4) _____ a company in (5) _____: Hoyu Shokai. But after the 1923 Great Kanto Earthquake and World War II, the company's survival was in danger. (6) _____ what did he do? He was a serious businessman who despised debt, but he asked distributors (7) _____ Japan to pre-pay for *Genroku*. This saved the company, and it was only possible because of the strong trust previously built with business partners.

● **companion** 仲間 ● **distributors** 販売業者

Step 4 ▶▶▶ Interaction

Make pairs and ask each other questions given below.

1. What is your favorite color and why?

2. What is the most expensive shopping you've done and why did you decide to purchase it?

Step 5 ▶▶▶ Summary & Presentation

Ⓠ 1. Summarize the passage by using the following keywords.

dye   color   innovative   product

dissolve   wants   dissatisfaction   field

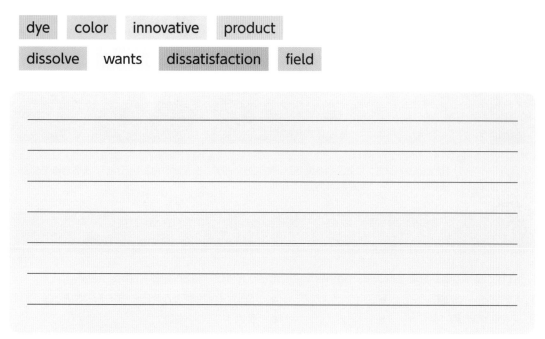

Ⓠ 2. Make a presentation of the summary made above.

Lesson 4

Japan Blue
— "Real and genuine" that never fades away

JAPAN BLUE CO.,LTD

🔊 **INTRODUCTION** 「桃太郎ジーンズ」で知られる同社が、地元児島のデニム産業の強みを活かし、ある特徴を前面に出しながらいかに躍進を続けているか？

Step 1 ▶▶▶ Vocabulary Buildup

Match the words and phrases below with the correct meanings in Japanese.

1. dozens of **1** ● ● （計画・プログラムを）実行する、遂行する
2. renown **2** ● ● 努力する、努める
3. possess **3** ● ● 流行している、広まっている
4. prevailing **4** ● ● 数十の〜、多数の〜
5. massive **5** ● ● 〜のおかげで
6. attribute A to B **5** ● ● 〜を持つ、有する
7. elevation **5** ● ● A を B のお陰だと考える
8. execute **5** ● ● （思想・文体などを）高尚にすること
9. modify **6** ● ● 大規模な、壮大な
10. endeavor **6** ● ● 〜に修正する、改造する
11. merge (with〜) **7** ● ● 名声
12. owing to **9** ● ● （〜と）統合する、合併させる

Reading

Audio 1-08

1 Kojima is an area of Kurashiki, Okayama Prefecture, 20 minutes southwest of Okayama Station by express train. Dozens of pairs of jeans hanging outside of Kojima Station turn heads. A short walk away is Jeans Street, where over 40 stores sell blue jeans and legions of fans of the attire congregate. This is a veritable jeans mecca, the home of their origin in Japan, and a major 5 production center.

2 Among the large concentration of jeans makers in Kojima, Japan Blue has earned international renown. In fact, many people seem to know about Japan Blue's uniquely named *Momotaro Jeans* brand, too.

創業者 真鍋寿男氏

3 The founder, Manabe Hisao, worked at 10 Kurashiki City Hall before taking a job with a textiles trading house. With the knowledge he gained there, at age 37, he founded a denim fabric distributor in 1992. Possessing a dream of bringing Japanese denim to the world that he still holds 15 today, Manabe leverages the strengths of the local denim production industry in Kojima. His dream appears to be nearing fruition.

4 Japan Blue, originally named Rampuya, launched its original *Momotaro Jeans* brand of products in 2006. It came in three types: *True Indigo Denim* (about 80,000 yen) sewn from true indigo-dyed yarn; *Organic Hand Denim* (about 40,000 yen) made with organically grown cotton; and *Momotaro Denim* (about 20,000 yen) sporting 20

ジャパンブルー本社 (岡山県倉敷市) 25

patches featuring the Japanese folk-tale hero Momotaro. Japan Blue started down a path completely opposite of the prevailing trend of competing on price by manufacturing in China and elsewhere overseas.

ポケットに桃太郎ののぼり旗を模した二本の白線は
桃太郎ジーンズの代表的特徴 (出陣レーベルジーンズ)

5 The massive growth the company experienced after the launch is attributable to placing front-and- 30 center the great added value of being "Made in Japan." Some especially notable characteristics include the reproduction of traditional indigo dyeing with synthetic indigo; the elevation of jeans to high

35

桃太郎ジーンズを織るのに欠かせない旧式力織機の豊田 GL9

40

45

fashion by replacing the denim's material with premium cotton, a world first; and skilled craftsmanship to execute fine sewing and attention to detail suited to sophisticated fashion.

6 Manabe wondered if Japan had invented jeans before America, whether they would have become indigo-dyed by hand like other traditional Japanese craftwork. So, he began building a loom. First, he installed a loom from Nishijin, a district of Kyoto with a long history of kimono production. The original loom was designed for weaving narrow silk strips from fine silk yarn, but Manabe modified it for thicker yarns and larger cotton fabrics. He then

50 hired a weaver. Thus, Manabe endeavored to carry on local craftsmanship by producing handwoven denim.

7 In 2014, Rampuya, a denim item manufacturer and distributor, merged with Collect Co., Ltd., a denim fabric design and distribution firm, to create Japan Blue Co., Ltd.

55 **8** Thanks to Manabe's brilliant thinking and leadership, Japan Blue has grown. But how is the company developing new jeans now? Japan Blue designs products with a sort of non-hierarchical collegiality. The company does not assign specific people to development roles. Rather, many different employees meet in open brainstorming sessions and engage in discussion to make

60 decisions. If a proposed product becomes a hit upon launch, the success fuels all employees' motivation toward the development process.

9 Japan Blue still sells completely handmade, indigo-dyed vintage items, but each pair costs upward of 200,000 yen. And yet their popularity is so great there

65 is a waiting list for buyers. Owing to the company's efforts, jeans have evolved into sophisticated Japanese fashion for personal enjoyment.

国内外の企業や学校関係者に向けて工場見学の受け入れを行っている

● l. 3 : **turn heads** 注意を引く、注目を集める ● l. 4 : **legions of** 多数の〜 ● l. 4 : **attire** 衣装、服装 ● l. 4 : **congregate** 集まる、群集する ● l. 5 : **veritable** 実際の、紛れもない ● l. 11 : **City Hall** 市役所 ● l. 12 : **textile** 織物の ● l. 13 : **fabric** 生地、織物 ● l. 18 : **nearing fruition** 実を結ぼうとしている ● l. 23 : **yarn** 織り糸、編み糸 ● ll. 26-27 : **start down a path** 道を歩み始める ● ll. 30-31 : **front-and-center** 中心の ● l. 34 : **synthetic** 合成の、人工の ● l. 44 : **loom** 織り機 ● l. 47 : **weave** 織る ● l. 57 : **non-hierarchical** 非階層的の ● l. 57 : **collegiality** 同僚との関係

step 2 ▶▶▶ Comprehension Questions

After reading the passage, choose either True (T), False (F), or "No information available in the passage"(?) for the statements below.

1. Jeans Street, a place near Kojima Station is the area for jeans fans. ( )

2. For the uniqueness of its name, *Momotaro Jeans* became famous. ( )

3. The price of the jeans in Japan Blue varied by the size and the color. ( )

4. The company changed their name due to the merging with other company in 2012. ( )

5. Japan Blue is now planning to sell non-handmade indigo-dyed items. ( )

step 3 ▶▶▶ One More Episode

🔊 Audio 1-09

Listen and fill in the blanks.

Kojima was originally an island before a ⁽¹⁾ _____ land reclamation project connected it to form large tracts of farmland, where cotton plants that can withstand the ⁽²⁾ _____ could be grown. Using the cotton, the local ⁽³⁾ _____ industry thrived and established Kojima's reputation as a ⁽⁴⁾ _____

児島の南端に位置する鷲羽山からの眺め

producer of cotton and apparel. ⁽⁵⁾ _____, the industry developed an array of techniques for using thick, sturdy fabric to produce clothing that must be long-lasting, such as school uniforms. These practices laid the ⁽⁶⁾ _____ for Kojima to create, in 1965, the first blue jeans made in Japan. Since then, a diverse ⁽⁷⁾ _____ of jeans manufacturers have set up shop in Kojima.

● **reclamation** 開拓・埋め立て ● **tract** (土地などの) 大きな広がり ● **thrive** (経済的に) 富む

step 4 ▶▶▶ Interaction

Make pairs and ask each other questions given below.

> 1. How would you dress up when playing outdoor and why?
> 2. What is the handmade product that you have or bought?

step 5 ▶▶▶ Summary & Presentation

Q 1. Summarize the passage by using the following keywords.

jeans   denim   manufacture   loom

craftmanship   leadership   brainstorm   handmade

_____

_____

_____

_____

_____

_____

Q 2. **Make a presentation** of the summary made above.

Goto
—— Making astronomy a business

 株式会社 五藤光学研究所

府中市郷土の森博物館 (東京都)

INTRODUCTION 天文をビジネスにするという、アイデアあふれる創業者の思いは、現在の五藤光学研究所に受け継がれている。「星とともに、技術とともに」同社が歩んだ歴史と挑戦とは？

▶▶▶ Vocabulary Buildup

Match the words and phrases below with the correct meanings in Japanese.

1.	planetarium **1**	●
2.	telescope **2**	●
3.	manufacturer **2**	●
4.	consistently **3**	●
5.	curiosity **4**	●
6.	astronomy **4**	●
7.	skilled **4**	●
8.	match A with B **4**	●
9.	anticipate **4**	●
10.	pioneer **5**	●
11.	expertise in **6**	●
12.	profound **6**	●
13.	genius **7**	●
14.	bathe in **7**	●

- ● A と B を一致させる
- ● プラネタリウム
- ● 好奇心、もの珍しさ
- ● 望遠鏡
- ● ～の専門的技術
- ● ～に浸す
- ● 熟練した、腕のいい
- ● 矛盾なく
- ● 深遠な、心からの
- ● 予期する、楽しみにして待つ
- ● 天才、特徴
- ● 製造業者、メーカー
- ● パイオニア、先駆者
- ● 天文学

Reading

Audio 1-10

1 What do you think of when you hear the word "planetarium"? Do you imagine a scientific instrument packed with astronomical discoveries, or perhaps a romantic place for a date?

5

10 創業当時の望遠鏡

2 Goto Inc. was founded in 1926 as Japan's only specialist telescope manufacturer. Thereafter, the company delivered telescopes to schools, science museums, and elsewhere all over Japan. Later, Goto started producing planetariums in Japan and developed a mass-production process for various models to become a top planetarium manufacturer.

3 The company's founder, Goto Seizo, wanted to create a company culture with a consistently research-oriented mindset, even if the company was small.

15

4 He was an inventor full of curiosity. Halley's Comet made a powerful impression on him when it passed by Earth during his childhood. At the age of 35, he went into the telescope business independently. His focus was on creating a business out of astronomy. Although he basically

20 創業者 五藤齋三氏

made what he wanted, Mr. Goto was skilled at matching it with demand, which is to say he could anticipate potential needs and produce something to show what those needs were.

5 Mr. Goto was quite impressed by planetariums when he visited astronomical observatories in America in 1955, so he

25 decided to build one in Japan. He then opened a dedicated factory and in 1959 developed the M-Class medium-sized planetarium. That year, gambling on the company's future, he set up the Goto Planetarium Hall, a special building at the Tokyo International Trade Fair. It became a popular

30 attraction. Because Goto's planetarium, which was a fraction of the price of a Carl Zeiss projector, was compact but outfitted with the features of a large one, Goto received inquiries from

レンズ投映式中型プラネタリウム
（M-1 型）

some 40 facilities. The company's first planetarium was installed on the roof of the Shin-Sekai Building in Tokyo's Asakusa district, and the second was

大阪万博「みどり館」

delivered to The Discovery Museum in Bridgeport, Connecticut in America. Goto took this opportunity to turn planetariums into a serious business. At Japan's first World Expo, held in Osaka in 1970, Goto developed the *Astrorama*, the world's first pan-hemispheric motion picture projection system, for the Midori-kan pavilion. The domed structure was a pioneering facility that led to orders from astronomical facilities and science museums from all corners.

6 Planetariums became Goto's core business thereafter, and now the company is a creator of fantastical spaces. Goto is proficient in projecting immersive images in real time across a domed screen through a perfect harmony between video projectors and a planetarium. Since Goto handles all the hardware, including dome design, lighting, audio equipment, seats, and so on, as well as production of planetarium shows, the company is both a planetarium maker and program producer. One point worth mentioning is that thanks to Goto's expertise in planetariums, the company can produce programs that present the entire night sky with astounding effects. In addition to covering the company's area of expertise in astronomy and outer space, Goto's shows are designed to explore deep into the wonder of science and the beauty of nature, using characters to tell an enjoyable story for audiences of all ages to learn something profound, experience thrills, and feel amazement.

プラネタリウム　港区立みなと科学館（東京都）

プラネタリウム　府中市郷土の森博物館（東京都）

7 Mr. Goto's dreams have certainly turned into reality. You, too, should experience the fantasy of his genius, gazing at the gorgeous starry sky under a dome as you are bathed in blissful sounds.

Notes

● l. 2 : **astronomical** 天文学的な ● l. 4 : **Inc.**（= incorporated 法人組織の）株式会社 ● l. 13 : **research-oriented** 研究志向の ● l. 14 : **mindset** 思考態度 ● l. 15 : **Halley's Comet** ハレー彗星 ● l. 24 : **observatory** 観測所、展望台 ● l. 25 : **dedicate** 〜を捧げる、献身する ● l. 31 : **Carl Zeiss** カール・ツァイス：ドイツの光学機器メーカー ● l. 31 : **outfit** 供給する (with)、備える ● l. 33 : **install** 〜に取り付ける ● l. 36 : **Bridgeport** ブリッジポート：アメリカ合衆国コネチカット州南西部に位置する都市 ● l. 40 : *Astrorama* アストロラマ：アストロ（天体）とドラマ（劇）の合成語。大型フィルムを複数台用いた全天全周映像装置のこと。 ● l. 41 : **pan-** 全〜、総〜 ● l. 41 : **hemispheric** 半球状の ● l. 42 : **Midori-kan** みどり館：大阪万博にあった展示館の一つ ● l. 47 : **fantastical spaces** 幻想的空間 ● l. 59 : **astounding** 仰天させるような、すごい ● l. 60 : **outer space** 宇宙

2 ▶▶▶ Comprehension Questions

After reading the passage, choose either True (T), False (F), or "No information available in the passage"(?) for the statements below.

1. Goto Inc. was the only specialist telescope manufacturer in Japan. (　　)

2. The founder was an inventor full of power and fame. (　　)

3. Mr. Goto decided to build a planetarium after visiting one in America. (　　)

4. Planetariums became a tiny but important part of the company's business.

(　　)

5. Goto's productions are designed to explore deep into the wonders of the world. (　　)

3 ▶▶▶ One More Episode

🔊 **Audio 1-11**

Listen and fill in the blanks.

Goto Seizo worked on the development of an "umbrella cooker" that used [superscript (1)] _____ and a solar heating and cooling system as well as [superscript (2)] _____. When he instructed his employees to produce a machine that automatically counts bills, because he foresaw the day when bank employees would [superscript (3)] _____ count money by hand, his workers came up with a bill bundle wrapping machine. Although the company never turned these devices [superscript (4)] _____ a business, it was clearly evident that Mr. Goto was a genius who saw the [superscript (5)] _____ for the trees to think one step ahead of everyone else.

● **a solar heating and cooling system** 太陽熱冷暖房システム ● **foresaw** (foresee「予見する、予測する」の過去形)

太陽熱冷暖房システムとは？ 屋根の傾斜面に複数個のトイ状の放物面鏡を設置し、これを水平面内で回転させて太陽を追尾させたシステムです。

step 4 ▶▶▶ Interaction

Make pairs and ask each other questions given below.

1. Which do you prefer: seeing the stars in a planetarium or outside at night? Why?
2. What is the best place for you to go to feel motivated? Why?

step 5 ▶▶▶ Summary & Presentation

Q 1. Summarize the passage by using the following keywords.

planetarium　founder　mindset　curiosity

needs　install　core　fantastical

Q 2. [Make a presentation] of the summary made above.

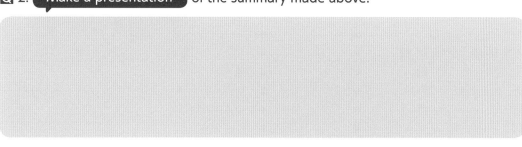

表紙・本文画像提供　五藤光学研究所

Lesson 6

Kanou Shojuan 叶匠寿庵
— Appreciating nature and culture

代表的な商品「あも」で知られる地元第一主義の企業が全国的な百貨店進出を果たし、さらに通販への進出等を実現させたプロセスとは？
INTRODUCTION

Step 1 ▶▶▶ Vocabulary Buildup

Match the words and phrases below with the correct meanings in Japanese.

1. confectionary **1** ● ● …を取り入れる
2. sensations **2** ● ● 直接
3. bound by **3** ● ● …を模倣する
4. turn ~ on its head **3** ● ● 感覚・知覚
5. mimic **3** ● ● 全国
6. in person **4** ● ● （…してほしいと）頼む
7. think highly of **4** ● ● ～をくつがえす
8. beg to (do) **4** ● ● 菓子店
9. reputation **4** ● ● 評判
10. nationwide **5** ● ● …に縛られる
11. adopt **5** ● ● …を尊重する

Reading

🔊 **Audio 1-12**

寿長生の郷
叶 匠壽庵の本社はこの
広大な施設内にある

1 Sunai no Sato, a plot of land in the mountains covering some 200,000 square meters in the Oishiryumon area of Otsu, Shiga Prefecture, is home to the headquarters and entire operation of Kanou Shojuan Co., Ltd., a seller of premium Japanese confectionaries to high-end department stores across Japan.

2 The company's name, Kanou Shojuan, consists of four Japanese characters, referring to "wishes coming true," (叶) "artisanal skill," (匠) "the joy of longevity," (壽) and "a nature retreat." (庵)

3 Kanou Shojuan started out in 1958 as a Japanese confectionery shop founded by Shibata Seiji, who was employed by the Otsu municipal tourism section. While at university, he had worked on writing scenarios, but he decided to produce gorgeous Japanese sweets rooted in the nature and seasonal sensations of Japan, as well as the history and culture of his home in Shiga. As a newcomer to the business, he was not bound by tradition, allowing him to invent new products through innovative thinking.

Shibata's use of individually wrapped sweets and product names were ahead of their time. For example, let's take his most well-known creation: *Amo*. It is a combination of *gyûhi* rice flour confectionary and fine *azuki* beans, but contrary to tradition, he put the *azuki* around the *gyûhi*. Turning convention on its head, *Amo* has a pleasantly unusual flavor because the *gyûhi* seeps out after the sweet *azuki*. The name "Amo" comes from the word for *mochi*, in the elegant speech used by the ladies of Japan's imperial court long ago.

叶 匠壽庵の代表銘菓「あも」

4 The business began with a small store in Otsu's Nagara neighborhood. When Echigo Masakazu, the fifth-generation president of Chu Itoh & Corporation and a Shiga native, heard about Kanou Shojuan's delectable offerings, he became a regular customer, visiting the shop in person. He, along with

35 other fellow businessmen from the Kansai region, such as Panasonic founder Matsushita Konosuke, thought highly of the confectionaries, which eventually became available at the Hankyu Department Store in Osaka's downtown Umeda district. This was a surprise, as department store purchasers had been visiting Nagara for eight years pleading to sell the sweets. Usually the case is

40 the exact opposite, with producers begging department stores to stock their items. Kanou Shojuan's high-end treats already had a stellar reputation, and when people found out they could easily get their hands on them at the department store, they formed huge lines for the opening. Six years later, the sweets appeared at the Seibu and Takashimaya department stores in Tokyo,

45 both managed by Shiga natives. Suddenly, Kanou Shojuan's products were for sale in department stores nationwide.

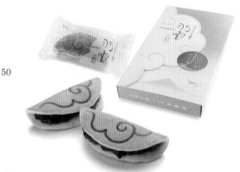

5 Rather than a top-down approach, Kanou Shojuan's third-generation and current president adopts a bottom-up style

50 by suggesting ideas, which the employees then consider and turn into products. Department store sales currently account for the majority of revenues, but the company has not been complacent. Kanou Shojuan is always coming up with new

55
羽田空港で限定販売の「羽雲」

ways to satisfy customers, for example, branching into mail-order sales and creating confectionary gifts only available at airports. While adapting its business management style, Kanou Shojuan values customers, flavors, nature, and culture above all else. It will be interesting to see what the future holds in

60 store for this enterprise.

Notes

● l. 2 : square meters 平方メートル ● l. 3 : headquarters 本社／本拠地 ● l. 7 : artisanal 職人 ● l. 20 : *gyûhi* 求肥・牛皮（ぎゅうひ）：和菓子の材料の一つで、白玉粉または餅粉に砂糖や水飴を加えて練りあげたもの ● l. 21 : contrary to …に反して ● l. 24 : seep out にじみ出る ● l. 26 : imperial court 朝廷 ● l. 31 : Chu Itoh & Corporation 伊藤忠商事株式会社：日本を代表する商社の1つで、1992年に英語社名を ITOCHU Corporation とした。● l. 32 : delectable おいしそうな ● l. 39 : plead 懇願する ● l. 41 : stellar reputation 素晴らしく高い評判 ● l. 47 : top-down approach トップダウン（上意下達）式の方法 ● l. 49 : bottom-up style ボトムアップ（下からの発議）式の方法 ● l. 58 : value 尊重する ● l. 59 : above all else 何をおいても ● ll. 59-60 : what the future holds in store 未来が待ち受けるもの

step 2 ▶▶▶ Comprehension Questions

After reading the passage, choose either True (T), False (F), or "No information available in the passage"(?) for the statements below.

1. Sunai no Sato is the previous name of the company and has four different meanings.   (   )
2. *Amo* was the first and the most well-known sweets.   (   )
3. The president of Chu Itoh & Corporation was a loyal customer.   (   )
4. It is uncommon for the department stores to be begged by the producers to stock their item.   (   )
5. The current president takes time to hear the employee's opinion about the new products.   (   )

step 3 ▶▶▶ One More Episode

Audio 1-13

Listen and fill in the blanks.

The man who took over the family business (1) ___ Sunai no Sato was even more innovative (2) _____ the founder because he embarked (3) ____ a grand project to produce sweets through a combination of agriculture and creation. Day in and day out, he produced

Japanese confectionaries here in his workshop from the plum blossom trees the company (4) _____ on its expansive grounds and many other homegrown

ingredients. He had a tearoom, teahouse, dining hall, and shop set up. The setting makes for an excellent place to take a stroll , attracting (5) _____ visitors a year. Now the company is taking on new challenges (6) _____ a bakery and café.

step 4 ▶▶▶ Interaction

Make pairs and ask each other questions given below.

> **1.** What is your favorite confectionary and why?
>
> **2.** What is your motto in life? Why?

step 5 ▶▶▶ Summary & Presentation

Q 1. Summarize the passage by using the following keywords.

| department stores | founder | nature | newcomer | *Amo* |
| regular customer | in person | beg | bottom-up | satisfy |

_____
_____
_____
_____
_____
_____

Q 2. **Make a presentation** of the summary made above.

Lesson 7

Kobayashi Pharmaceutical
—— What is the fountain of their good ideas?

小林製薬株式会社

INTRODUCTION

「あったらいいな」をカタチにする——CM でおなじみの同社の戦略は「小さな池の大きな魚」という
うもの。大きな池は皆が来るから競争が激しく、なかなか釣れない。でも、小さな池では、人があ
まり来ず競争がないため、魚を独占できる。つまり「ニッチ商品による新市場創造」がそれである。

step 1 ▶▶▶ Vocabulary Buildup

Match the words and phrases below with the correct meanings in Japanese.

1. along with **1** ●   ● ～を生む
2. medication **1** ●   ● 長続きする
3. generate **2** ●   ● 収穫する、収集する
4. harvest **2** ●   ● ひらめき、素晴らしい思い付き
5. inspiration **4** ●   ● 薬剤、医薬
6. long-lasting **4** ●   ● 協力する
7. literally **4** ●   ● 収益
8. novel **5** ●   ● 新しい
9. revenue **5** ●   ● 文字どおり（に）
10. collaborate **6** ●   ● ～と共に

Reading

Audio 1-14

1 Not a day goes by when a commercial from Kobayashi Pharmaceutical doesn't appear on TV. Along with medications, the commercials introduce fragrances, air fresheners, skincare products, sanitary items, and various other daily household goods. What they all
5 share in common is the good impression they have. One might make people think, "What a great idea!" or "These guys come up with such novel ideas!" As one can tell from the company's brand slogan, "You
10 make a wish and we make it happen," this is exactly what the company is going for.

アイデアプレゼンの様子

2 The biggest reason why Kobayashi Pharmaceutical's net sales and profits have continued to rise is the enthusiasm and speed with which the company enters new markets through product development. In a company with some
15 3,000 employees on a consolidated basis, those workers generate over 35,000 ideas a year. Some departments produce more ideas than others, but essentially, no matter what department an employee is stationed in, he or she is asked to come up with at least one suggestion a month. This instills a habit of taking notes about daily inconveniences and troubles that could lead to new
20 ideas. If one of them is taken up and it leads to a new product launch, the employee who came up with it receives a bonus. This system provides considerable motivation. Of course, in addition to harvesting the ideas of its employees, Kobayashi Pharmaceutical frequently conducts interviews with end users of its products.

25

30

商品パッケージの男の子、熱さまくんは
初代ブランドマネージャー（現国際事業部
長）の宮西一仁氏がモデルだった。

3 The story of hit product *Netsu-sama Sheet* provides a good example of how the employee idea-generation process works. When it was launched in 1994, it was a smash, selling 5.5 million units a year.

4 The inspiration came from an employee who said that when a child has a fever, preparing a cold towel to bring it down is troublesome. Subsequent market research found heavy demand for an item that is easy to use, stays in place, and has a long-lasting effect. A member of the product development team was vexed by an inability to

find a material meeting the requirements, but one day at a pub, a solution 35
literally fell into her hand: *sashimi konnyaku* that is cold to the touch!

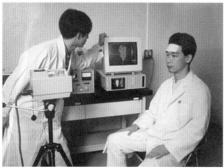

研究開発の様子

5 After much trial and error, Kobayashi Pharmaceutical came up with an idea for a non-woven fabric coated with a cooling gel. The product followed thereafter. However, 40 how could the company give consumers an accurate picture of exactly what this novel product was? They came up with a straightforward name: *Netsu-sama Sheet*. The package 45

also has an illustration of a feverish boy with a sheet on his forehead. These decisions, along with a clear message delivered through TV commercials, made the product a rousing success upon its launch. Later, people also started using *Netsu-sama Sheet* as a way to beat the summer heat. Now available in about 50

発売時の熱さまシート

20 overseas markets, it continues to bring in steady revenues for the company.

6 Kobayashi Pharmaceutical is a firm that:

1. pools ideas from throughout the company to identify potential consumer needs,
2. thoroughly investigates those needs to 55 develop what consumers want,
3. collaborates in teams to research and develop quality products, and
4. engages in effective communication through product naming, packaging, and commercials. 60

A strict adherence to this approach makes Kobayashi Pharmaceutical an exemplary BtoC enterprise.

ブランドマネージャーの西浦由香利氏と熱さまくん

Notes

● l. 12 : net sales 純売上高 ● l. 15 : consolidated basis 連結ベース ● l. 17 : stationed ～に就いている ● l. 18 : instill （主義・思想などを）教え込む、植え付ける ● l. 23-24 : end users （製品の）末端使用者 ● l. 28 : smash 大成功、大ヒット ● l. 34 : vexed イライラした、困った ● l. 37 : trial and error 試行錯誤 ● l. 39 : non-woven 不織の ● l. 40 : thereafter それ以来 ● l. 48 : rousing success 満足のいく成功 ● l. 49 : upon ～すると すぐに ● l. 61 : adherence （規則などの）順守 ● l. 62 : BtoC　Business to Consumer：企業が個人に対して商品・サービスを提供する取引

step 2 ▶▶▶ Comprehension Questions

After reading the passage, choose either True (T), False (F), or "No information available in the passage"(?) for the statements below.

1. Kobayashi Pharmaceutical appears in TV commercials every day. (　)

2. The company grows even without the speed of product development. (　)

3. *Netsu-sama Sheet* was produced by one of the new employees. (　)

4. The consumers can easily understand the product by use of visual aids. (　)

5. The company is always developing products which customers wish to have.

(　)

step 3 ▶▶▶ One More Episode

🔊 **Audio 1-15**

Listen and fill in the blanks.

Although most people who know Kobayashi Pharmaceutical think of it as a company in Osaka, its origins (1) _____ to Nagoya, when Kobayashi Chubei opened Kobayashi Seidaido, a store selling cosmetics and general merchandise, in (2) _____. When Mr. Kobayashi expanded his business to Osaka, his main business was wholesaling pharmaceuticals, but (3) _____ of the thin profit margins, he decided to (4) _____ the enterprise into a manufacturer engaged in production and sales. In a field crowded with other big drugmakers, what he needed to

小林製薬本社 (大阪府大阪市)

(5) _____ them was "meticulous product development." The resulting surge (6) _____ has been remarkable, as the company has (7) _____ with one hit product after another.

● **origin** 起源 ● **profit margins** 利益率 (利益÷売上高) ● **meticulous** 細心の

step 4 ▶▶▶ Interaction

Make pairs and ask each other questions given below.

1. When you feel ill, what do you usually do to feel better and why?
2. Do you like studying collaboratively in a group or individually? Why?

step 5 ▶▶▶ Summary & Presentation

🔊 Audio 2-25

Q 1. Summarize the passage by using the following keywords.

| medications | develop | employees | idea |
| inconvenience | selling | product | overseas |

_____

_____

_____

_____

_____

_____

_____

Q 2. **Make a presentation** of the summary made above.

Lesson 8

Takamine
—— The pioneer of acoustic electric guitar

INTRODUCTION 自社ブランド「Takamine」の立ち上げ、カマーン・ミュージック社と提携、エレアコの開発、挑戦を続ける同社の原点にあるものとは？

step 1 ▶▶▶ Vocabulary Buildup

Match the words and phrases below with the correct meanings in Japanese.

1. inspire **2**	●	● 優良な、素晴らしい
2. affection **2**	●	● 押し上げ、向上
3. distributor **3**	●	● 鼓舞する
4. struggle to do **4**	●	● A に B を提供する
5. provide A with B **4**	●	● 〜の割合を占める
6. component **4**	●	● 長期の
7. boost **5**	●	● （機械・ステレオの）部品
8. initially **5**	●	● 優しい思い、愛情
9. thanks to **6**	●	● 株主
10. account for **7**	●	● もがく、努力する
11. shareholder **7**	●	● 分配者
12. long-term **7**	●	● 初めのうちは
13. prime **7**	●	● …のお陰で

Bruce Springsteen と Jon Bon Jovi の使用ギターとして有名な EF341SC

Reading

Kotaro Oshio 押尾コータロー／
Acoustic Guitarist

Sakurako Ohara 大原櫻子／
Singer・Actress

1 The guitar is a musical instrument that delivers the fun of music to people worldwide, whether rock, pop, folk, or classical. Takamine Gakki Co., Ltd., a standout guitar maker selling instruments in 64 countries, is a favorite among top Japanese musicians like Nagabuchi Tsuyoshi, Oshio Kotaro, The Yellow Monkey, Kitagawa Yujin of Yuzu, and Ohara Sakurako, along with global stars 5 such as Bruce Springsteen, Bruno Mars, and Jon Bon Jovi.

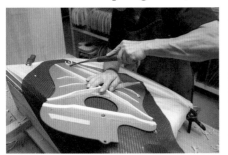

表板裏面に、補強のための力板（響棒）を装着し、ギターのモデルに合わせてノミで力板を削りながら調整する様子。熟練を要する作業の一つ。

2 The company is located in Nakatsugawa, southeastern Gifu Prefecture. The founder, Ozone Kai'ichiro, learned to make stringed instruments in Nagoya. In September 1959, 10 he moved in with his wife's family after a giant typhoon in Ise Bay caused damage to the Tokai region. That December, he started a company, Ozone Gakki Ltd. At first, it produced classical guitars for performers of 15 that era's mainstream *enka* ballads. The company's renamed itself Takamine Gakki Ltd. in 1962 and incorporated in 1965. The name of the company and brand was inspired by the elegant Mt. Takamine, a local symbol, out of great affection for the community.

3 The company's own Takamine brand came out in the late 20 1970s. Around then, the company partnered with Kaman Music, a major American instrument distributor, to export guitars. This was a big step forward for Takamine. Charles Kaman, president of helicopter manufacturer Kaman Corporation, established Kaman Music as a group company in 1966. A guitar enthusiast, 25 Mr. Kaman applied acoustic measurement and analysis techniques to develop guitars made with the same glass fiber found in helicopter parts. These instruments would later become the Ovation brand.

カマーン社と提携した当時のギター

4 As concerts became bigger in the 1970s, professional musicians struggled to 30 produce powerful yet beautiful sounds from acoustic guitars. Kaman Music provided a solution with an acoustic electric guitar outfitted with a pickup, a component to capture the sound, in the bridge. Professional American musicians were quick to take it up, and Kaman Music began selling both its

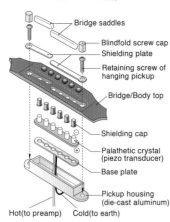

パラセティック・ピックアップの
各パーツの名称

Bridge saddles
Blindfold screw cap
Shielding plate
Retaining screw of
hanging pickup
Bridge/Body top
Shielding cap
Palathetic crystal
(piezo transducer)
Base plate
Pickup housing
(die-cast aluminum)
Hot(to preamp)   Cold(to earth)

35

40

45

50

Ovation brand and Takamine guitars imported from Japan in the US market.

5 Takamine started developing its own acoustic electric guitar in 1978. The company put out the *Palathetic Pickup*, which was better than other pickups at capturing rich sounds even under loud conditions. Famous acts like The Eagles started performing with Takamine acoustic electric guitars, boosting the brand's reputation. Although the Japanese market initially resisted acoustic electric guitars with an electro component, the positive feedback overseas helped the company start selling the products in Japan a few years later. Many Japanese guitarists began playing Takamines.

6 The starting point for the company's product development is understanding what professional musicians on the cutting edge of the changing music scene want, then giving it to them. Thanks to trust built over many years, Takamine can test new products and get feedback on improvements from musicians at rehearsal studios and concert sound checks. That's how the company keeps making consumer guitars that are accessible and sound amazing.

7 Employees happen to account for the largest proportion of Takamine shareholders, at 60%. The company's success hinges on the contributions of individual employees, who then see it in their bonuses and dividends. This arrangement motivates workers to grow even more. A company that enjoys long-term growth has a system comprising managers who act on the public's needs and the employees with their knowledge and passion. Takamine is a prime example.

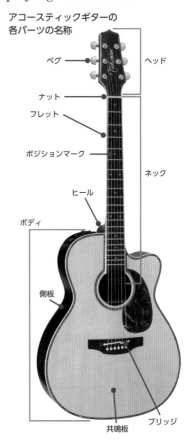

アコースティックギターの
各パーツの名称

ペグ / ヘッド / ナット / フレット / ポジションマーク / ネック / ヒール / ボディ / 側板 / 共鳴板 / ブリッジ

Notes

● l. 3 : **standout** 目立つ、際立つ ● l. 12 : **Ise Bay** 伊勢湾 ● l. 16 : **mainstream** 主流 ● l. 17 : **incorporate** 会社組織にする ● l. 21 : **Kaman Music** Kaman Music 社：有名ブランド・ギターの販売を手掛けている米国の企業 ● l. 26 : **acoustic** 音響の ● l. 32 : **pickup** ギターの弦振動を拾うマイクのような役割をしている部分 ● l. 41 : **act** グループ、バンド ● l. 52 : **the cutting edge** 最前線 ● l. 62 : **hinge on** ～次第である ● l. 64 : **dividends** 株式・保険の配当（金）

Step 2 ▶▶▶ Comprehension Questions

After reading the passage, choose either True (T), False (F), or "No information available in the passage"(?) for the statements below.

1. The founder learned how to make instruments in Nagoya, where the company is located. (　)
2. The company renamed itself in 1962, inspired by the mountain. (　)
3. In 1970, musicians fought against production of the acoustic electric guitar. (　)
4. It was in 1978 that Takamine started making their own electric guitars. (　)
5. About three-fifths of the employees are shareholders in the company. (　)

Step 3 ▶▶▶ One More Episode

🔊 Audio 1-17

Listen and fill in the blanks.

The Sakashita neighborhood of Nakatsugawa, a city in Gifu Prefecture, has rich resources of lumber (1) _____, such as Kiso cypress, but this wood is not well-suited for making guitars. (2) _____ said, carpentry work, such as building wooden buckets, was (3) _____ a prosperous business in Sakashita, so the wealth (4) ____ skilled woodworkers has been a boon to Takamine. By the way, have you (5) _____ heard the song "Hotel California" by The Eagles, a band that was mentioned in the reading passage? Glenn Frey played the intro to the song (6) _____ a Takamine guitar.

● **lumber** 材木 ● **that being said** そうは言っても ● **boon** 恩恵

step 4 ▶▶▶ Interaction

Make pairs and ask each other questions given below.

> 1. What kind of the music (e.g. ballads or popular music or *enka*) do you like listening to and why?
> 2. What do you do in your free time? Why?

step 5 ▶▶▶ Summary & Presentation

Q 1. Summarize the passage by using the following keywords.

worldwide   classical guitar   renamed   export

American   import   developing   product

高峰山 (標高 944.7m)

_____

_____

_____

_____

_____

_____

_____

Q 2. **Make a presentation** of the summary made above.

Lesson 9

ISHIYA
—— Delicate artisan cookies from Hokkaido

白い恋人パーク中庭（ローズガーデン）

石屋製菓の「白い恋人」は、今や日本のお土産として海外の旅行客からも人気の商品である。
同社は新作スイーツの販売にも余念がない。この独自のビジネスモデル確立の秘訣とは？

step 1 ▶▶▶ Vocabulary Buildup

Match the words and phrases below with the correct meanings in Japanese.

1.	associate **1**	● ●	A から B を連想する（A with B）
2.	souvenir **1**	● ●	需要
3.	found **2**	● ●	創設する
4.	keep up with **2**	● ●	目立った
5.	demand **2**	● ●	手につく、べとべとする
6.	sticky **3**	● ●	～を主張する
7.	struggle **5**	● ●	格闘する、苦しむ
8.	assert **5**	● ●	お土産品
9.	hail **5**	● ●	お菓子
10.	conspicuous **6**	● ●	～に追いつく
11.	executive **7**	● ●	至福の
12.	confectionery **8**	● ●	（～の理由で）好意的に受け入れる（for ～）
13.	blissful **8**	● ●	役員

Reading

1 Many people associate Hokkaido souvenirs with tasty *Shiroi Koibito* cookies. They contain a layer of chocolate wedged between crisp *langue de chat*. The producer and seller of this well-renowned snack is Sapporo-based Ishiya.

2 The company's history began in 1947, when Ishimizu Yukiyasu founded the
5　business to process starch for Japan's government. At first, he made children's snacks. In 1976, the company began selling *Shiroi Koibito*. They became a major hit and because production could not keep up with demand, for a while, daily operations extended well into the night.

3 Earlier, another company had success with a
10　new white chocolate product. As Ishiya experimented with its own offering, Mr. Ishimizu's son and then-CEO, Isao, wondered how he could make it simpler to eat the chocolate that melted easily and made hands sticky. Since it was so delicious
15　and easy to eat, the company tried placing the chocolate between *langue du chat*, an earlier product Ishiya was already selling. Each were delectable on their own, but the combination created new value.

4 Sales were at first limited to Hokkaido,
20　but when Isao pitched *Shiroi Koibito* to All Nippon Airways (ANA), they were served with in-flight meals on a Sapporo-to-Tokyo flight for two weeks beginning in October 1977. Word
25　spread about delicious snacks only travelers to Hokkaido could get. Even now, over 40 years later, Ishiya has no permanent shops outside Hokkaido

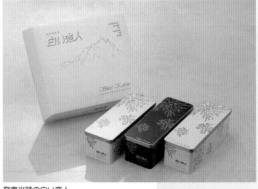

発売当時の白い恋人

selling *Shiroi Koibito*. This shows how important the association between the
30　cookies and their home prefecture is to the company.

5 The beautiful name *Shiroi Koibito* comes from how Yukiyasu once described falling snow to his son. He said, "White lovers fell down." This moment inspired Isao, who had been struggling to think up a name for the product. Some assert a connection with the film *13 Days in France*, a documentary

about the 1968 Grenoble Winter Olympics. More than just a documentary, the ³⁵
movie was hailed for its artistry and may have been inspired by director
Ichikawa Kon's *Tokyo Olympiad*.

6 The company also wanted the package
to represent snow falling from a blue sky,
but many competing products already ⁴⁰
had white packaging, so Ishiya made the
snowflakes more conspicuous with a dark
blue background. Thus, *Shiroi Koibito*
became a symbolic souvenir in Japan.

7 Ishiya's workforce is young, led by the ⁴⁵
founder's grandson, Ishimizu Hajime.
It's a company ready for any challenge.
Office workers have no assigned seats. Even the CEO lacks his own office! He
chats with all sorts of employees, not just executives. A visitor may see an
entry-level worker engaging in casual conversation with the CEO or a director. ⁵⁰
This openness is wonderfully invigorating for both management and labor,
leading to new ideas.

8 In 2017, the company opened its
first store outside Hokkaido, the
Ishiya Ginza, and now has six locations
outside the prefecture, including Tokyo's
Shinjuku district and Shinsaibashi in
Osaka. None of them sell *Shiroi Koibito*,
but they do offer new confectionery
creations crafted from years of
experience and skill and imbued with
a love for Hokkaido. They represent

ISHIYA GINZA 店舗（東京都）

⁵⁵

⁶⁰

the company's extraordinary motivation. Ishiya aspires to "Sweets that create
happiness," so it will be interesting to see what blissful combinations of flavors
are forthcoming. ⁶⁵

2 ▶▶▶ Comprehension Questions

After reading the passage, choose either True (T), False (F), or "No information available in the passage"(?) for the statements below.

1. Ishiya has a long history dating back to the beginning of the Meiji era. (   )

2. Isao is a grandson of the founder of Ishiya. (   )

3. The association between the snack and its home prefecture is a vital thing to Ishiya. (   )

4. Another company selling white chocolate products stopped selling them. (   )

5. Ishiya is a relatively young company, ready for any challenges. (   )

3 ▶▶▶ One More Episode

🔊 Audio 2-02

Listen and fill in the blanks.

In (1) _____, the company opened the Ishiya Chocolate Factory, a confectionery theme park, at its Sapporo head office. Renamed "Shiroi Koibito Park" in (2) _____, it is now a major Hokkaido tourist magnet. Visitors can tour the *Shiroi Koibito* production line, learn the history of chocolate, munch (3) ____

白い恋人パークのからくり時計塔

original sweets at the café, and take in the gardens. Illuminations light up the park in winter (4) ____ an even more incredibly stimulating experience for visitors of all ages. While boosting the appeal of the product and the company, the (5) _____ park popularizes confectioneries and helps stimulate Hokkaido's economy.

● **magnet** 人を惹きつけるもの ● **munch** むしゃむしゃ食べる

step 4 ▶▶▶ Interaction

Make pairs and ask each other questions given below.

> 1. What local sweets or food can you recommend to your partner and why?
> 2. What can you do to promote openness in a workplace?

step 5 ▶▶▶ Summary & Presentation

Q 1. Summarize the passage by using the following keywords.

| a major hit | sticky | *langue du chat* | in-flight meals |
| permanent shops | package | *Shiroi Koibito* | openness |

_____

_____

_____

_____

_____

_____

_____

Q 2. **Make a presentation** of the summary made above.

JustSystems

—— How the system made our life easier

INTRODUCTION 長年にわたり日本語変換にこだわり、膨大な辞書と用例を蓄積し、ユーザーの意見・要望を真摯に受け止めてきた ATOK の歴史とさらなる挑戦。

 1 ▶▶▶ Vocabulary Buildup

Match the words and phrases below with the correct meanings in Japanese.

1. foresee **2**　　　　　●　　　　●　出現
2. advent **2**　　　　　●　　　　●　進展する
3. convert to **2**　　　●　　　　●　切り替える
4. evolve **2**　　　　　●　　　　●　〜を真摯に受け止める
5. equip with **2**　　　●　　　　●　購入する
6. purchase **3**　　　　●　　　　●　迅速な
7. cut down **4**　　　　●　　　　●　備える、設備する
8. prompt **4**　　　　　●　　　　●　献身
9. dedication **5**　　　●　　　　●　削減する
10. take ~ seriously **5**　●　　　　●　予知する、見越す

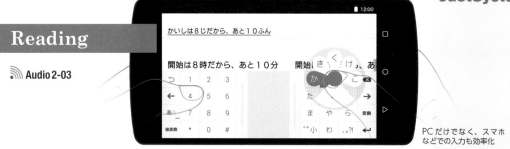

Reading

📶 Audio 2-03

PC だけでなく、スマホ
などでの入力も効率化

1 Before Windows and Macs, business computers were large, expensive machines that processed Japanese poorly, could only input limited characters, and required a great deal of time and effort for writing.

2 In 1979, software developer and distributor JustSystems was founded in Tokushima, and incorporated in 1981. Foreseeing the advent of the personal computer, the company recognized a future need for a simple system to input *kana* and convert to *kanji*, so JustSystems developed a Japanese input system. The unveiling of a Japanese processing system, the Kana-Kanji Transfer Input System (KTIS), at a 1982 Tokyo exhibition was a smash. The next year, NEC developed a PC with JustSystems' word processing software, JS-Word, powered by KTIS. KTIS then evolved into the more powerful Advanced Technology Of Kana-kanji transfer (ATOK) Japanese input system. In the early 1980s, as prices had come down dramatically, many Japanese households purchased dedicated word processing machines that made processing Japanese easier and were equipped with a printing function. Then in 1985, JustSystems launched *Ichitaro*, a standalone word processing program for PCs. This convenient tool was a major hit for its powerful Japanese conversion and simple production of expressive text. JustSystems came up with the now standard feature which uses the spacebar to convert Japanese. The company later sold the software's ATOK feature as a standalone product and gradually upgraded *Ichitaro*. While Japanese people still preferred word processing machines for producing documents due to their wider array of keys and printing function, the

(line numbers: 5, 10, 15, 20, 25, 30, 35)

ATOK の便利な機能

おせわに
お世話になっております。
お世話に
　：
選択：Tab
先頭候補確定：Shift＋Enter　　推測候補

推測変換
入力し始めたときも入力し続ける
ときも、変換したいことばを先回
りして提示。

かくにんしました
確認しました
確定：Shift＋Enter　　復元候補

入力支援
入力中のミスを自動で修復。
タイプミスも、変換作業でなかっ
たことに。

社長が申しました《敬語の誤り》
社長がおっしゃいました
社長が仰いました
選択：↑↓
先頭候補確定：Shift＋Enter　　訂正候補
■解説表示：End

校正支援
同音語・重ね言葉・くだけた表現
の使用や、敬語・慣用句・ことわ
ざの誤用などを指摘。

表現モード
ATOK では、さまざまな方言を、そのままのことば（音）で入力できる。

表現モード	変換例(1)	変換例(2)
関西	めちゃ高いねん	見えへんやんか
北海道東北	湯っこさ入るべか	一緒に行がねが
関東	行くべー	あおなじみ
中部北陸	ケッタで行こまい	明日休みだもんで
中国四国	食べてみんさい	じゃけえねえ
九州	今日もよか天気ばい	何ばしよっと

顔文字
ATOK では、顔文字も
「ばんざい」から入力できる。

Λ
＼(^o^)／
1 banzai ⊞英字 ▸
2 Banzai ⊞英字 ▸
3 BANZAI ⊞英字 ▸
4 ＼(^o^)／ ▸
5 ＼(^_^)／ ▸
6 ＼(^o^)／ ▸
7 ＼(^.^)／ ▸
8 ＼(-o-)／ ▸
9 ＼(^0^)／ ▸
13/21 🔍 ▤
0 バンザイ,バンザイ… カタカナ・英字

combination of *Ichitaro* and ATOK was faster, smarter, and easier to use.

3 In 1995, the PC boom exploded when Microsoft released Windows 95. It was all
40 downhill from here for word processing machines as PCs took the spotlight. Computers running Windows came standard with Microsoft's Japanese conversion system, the Input Method Editor
45 (Microsoft IME), while many were sold with Word, the word processing software from the Microsoft Office suite, pre-installed. This was a blow for JustSystems, but even now there were still many users
50 who continue to purchase ATOK.

4 Why? Because the conversion is smart and fast. When you begin typing and as you continue to do so, the software anticipates and shows you the text or words you want
55 to convert to. If you make a typo, the software guesses what you really wanted to type, points it out, and even performs the conversion. This cuts down on editing and interrupted trains of thought. When you input an unregistered word in combination with other words, ATOK will prompt you to save the new word. All
60 you have to do is press Shift+Enter. It's an incredibly useful feature!

5 ATOK's success comes from years of dedication to converting the Japanese language, packaging the software with massive dictionaries and examples, and always taking user feedback seriously. The developers also write in Japanese and understand what problems users face, so in addition to direct input sent by
65 e-mail or telephone, they focus on researching comments in social media and blogs and conducting surveys to keep upgrading ATOK's features.

6 JustSystems, a Japanese company for the Japanese language, will hopefully keep building on its impressive track record.

変換候補にないことばを変換できるようにする
ひろあきから博昭の場合

1. 「ひろあき」と入力します。

ひろあき

2. スペースキーを押して変換します。

宏明

3. 変換をBackspaceキーで取り消します。

ひろあき

4. 「ひろあき」を「はかせ」に入力しなおし、「博士」に変換、確定します。

博士

5. Backspaceキーで「士」を削除します。

博

6. 続けて「しょうわ」と入力し、「昭和」と変換、確定します。

博昭和

7. Backspaceで「和」を削除すると「博昭」を学習するかどうかツールチップを表示します。

博昭

「ひろあき」から【博昭】に変換できるようにしますか？
学習する：Shift+Enter
修正して単語登録：Ctrl+F7

博昭

「ひろあき」から【博昭】に変換できるようにしますか？
学習する：Shift+Enter
修正して単語登録：Ctrl+F7

Notes

● l. 2 : characters 文字 ● l. 8 : unveiling 初公開 ● ll. 8-9 : Kana-Kanji Transfer Input System (KTIS) かな漢字変換ソフトウェア ● ll. 16-17 : dedicated word processing machine ワープロ専用機 ● l. 21 : standalone 単体 ● l. 24 : conversion 変換 ● l. 34 : array 配列 ● l. 40 : downhill 落ち目 ● ll. 44-45 : Input Method Editor (IME) 日本語入力ソフト：パソコンに日本語を入力するときは、キーボードから「かな入力」か「ローマ字入力」でひらがなを切り替えて入力することができ、それを漢字やカタカナなどを含む文章に変換するが、この変換の役割を担うのが IME ● l. 48 : blow 打撃 ● l. 55 : typo タイプミス、打ち間違え：typographical error の略 ● l. 58 : interrupt さえぎる、中断する ● l. 58 : trains of thought 一連の考え ● l. 68 : track record 実績

step 2 ▶▶▶ Comprehension Questions

After reading the passage, choose either True (T), False (F), or "No information available in the passage"(?) for the statements below.

1. In 1979, KTIS was the only system used for typewriters.   (   )

2. JustSystems developed KTIS before the hit of a personal computer.   (   )

3. KTIS is the advanced version of ATOK, with various new functions.   (   )

4. It took 10 years to upgrade *Ichitaro* after it was launched.   (   )

5. JustSystems is a company for helping foreigners learn Japanese.   (   )

step 3 ▶▶▶ One More Episode

🔊 **Audio 2-04**

Listen and fill in the blanks.

JustSystems has released many excellent programs in (1) _____ to ATOK and *Ichitaro*. One growth area of late is educational software. In (2) _____, the company offered elementary schools a program it had developed for classes (3) _____ computer labs. This was *Ichitaro Smile*, a Japanese word processing program (4) _____ elementary students. It comes with a version of ATOK that

せなかの かたむき

adjusts the sophistication of *kanji* conversion to each grade level. Students can learn (5) _____ to type text and create a newspaper. The software was (6) _____ renamed "Just Smile." Today, 85% of Japanese elementary schools use this program.

● **of late** 最近の ● **adjust** 調整する ● **sophistication** 洗練度

step 4 ▶▶▶ Interaction

Make pairs and ask each other questions given below.

1. When you use the computer, do you prefer to type in Japanese *kana* layout or English (QWERTY)layout? why?
2. Do you know any useful keyboard shortcut? If yes, what?

step 5 ▶▶▶ Summary & Presentation

Q 1. Summarize the passage by using the following keywords.

software   develop   input system   evolved

ATOK   conversion   typo   success

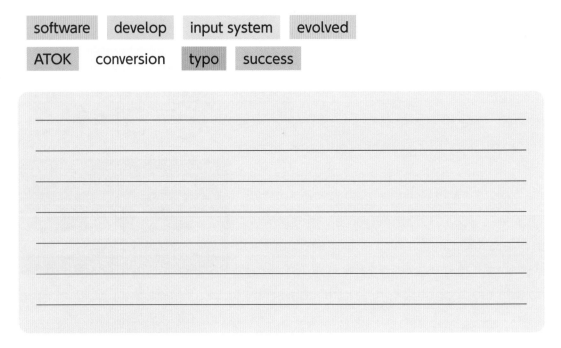

Q 2. Make a presentation of the summary made above.

Iwasaki

—— Attract your appetite as close as true to life

INTRODUCTION　本物そっくりの「食品サンプル」事業を日本で初めて企業化した同社が、飲食店の「総合プロデューサー」となるまでの軌跡を追う。

Step 1 ▶▶▶ Vocabulary Buildup

Match the words and phrases below with the correct meanings in Japanese.

1.	overwhelm **2**	●	●	外食する
2.	unaccustomed **4**	●	●	固める
3.	dine out **4**	●	●	顧客数
4.	feel at ease **4**	●	●	不慣れな
5.	client base **5**	●	●	驚くほど
6.	elaborate **5**	●	●	精密な、正確な
7.	inject **6**	●	●	精巧な
8.	harden **6**	●	●	壊れやすい
9.	stunningly **6**	●	●	気持ちが和む、安心する
10.	manufacture **7**	●	●	圧倒する
11.	precise **7**	●	●	製造する
12.	fragile **8**	●	●	～に注入する

Reading

ビーフステーキのサンプル

🔊 Audio 2-05

1 Surely you've experienced the delight of a colorful *bento* containing carefully placed, multihued ingredients that whet your appetite. Just as much as the flavor, traditional Japanese food made from natural ingredients is also enjoyable for its appearance.

5 **2** As Japan's economy grew after World War II, new restaurants opened serving Western and Chinese dishes. The foreign names on menus overwhelmed customers because their taste was unknown. But with a display case of plastic food samples, customers could immediately understand what was available. They also made customers hungrier and the food selection process more fun.

10 **3** Iwasaki Co., Ltd. founder Iwasaki Takizo made plastic food samples a big business. They were invented in Japan in or around the 1920s and first displayed on the dining floor of Shirokiya (the predecessor to Hankyu Department Store) in 1923.

創業者 岩崎瀧三氏

4 The samples made consumers who were unaccustomed to 15 dining out feel at ease. Mr. Iwasaki first saw them as a child. He loved dropping wax into water to make flower-like blossoms, and he was sure the replicas were wax. Food samples were still rare, so their mere presence boosted restaurant sales. Later, Mr. 20 Iwasaki founded a food sample company to make them commonplace throughout Japan. His wife, Suzu, helped him experiment with production methods before finding the right one.

食品サンプル第一号「記念オム」(1932 年)

5 Iwasaki's models were so impressive the 25 competition couldn't hold a candle to them. His talents at drawing and fine color adjustments helped. Mr. Iwasaki founded Iwasaki Seisakusho in Osaka in 1932 and began supplying the Sogo department store with its restaurants' first food models. Iwasaki then expanded its client base with restaurants who recognized the company's skills. In 1952, Iwasaki expanded to Tokyo. The 30 business was one beneficiary of the restaurant boom accompanying the 1964 Tokyo Olympics. In the 1980s, a switch from wax to synthetic resin allowed for more elaborate samples and dramatically higher productivity.

6 So how are food samples made? To begin production, employees carefully examine the restaurant and its food. Anything new is made from scratch with

食品サンプルの製作工程
完成したサンプル（写真6）は実物と
見分けがつかないほどそっくり

silicon. Plastic with the same color as the food is injected into the silicon. Then, ₃₅ it is hardened with heat and removed. The coloring creates stunningly realistic models so picture-perfect you can't tell them from the real thing. You could say a food sample factory is more like a studio of artists.

7 Iwasaki manufactures replicas that follow the customer's request to the letter. Different customers want different things, and chefs often ask for ₄₀ precise details. If the model looks much better than the original, or if it doesn't appear tasty and deters customers, Iwasaki may receive a complaint. Producing an exact replica of the real thing and making it look even tastier than the original is a delicate task.

8 Iwasaki also handmakes complex samples including life-size whales, alpine ₄₅ vegetation, things that normally melt or pop such as ice cream and beer

bubbles, and sensitive items like leather or handicrafts. Other creations include models for signs, menus, flyers, direct marketing items, food utensils, and in- ₅₀ store fixtures, making the company a general producer satisfying all the promotional needs of restaurants.

学術的にも評価された全長15m 全翼15mのザトウ鯨の模型

9 Beginning with replicas for department store dining floors, Iwasaki has since become an essential partner for restaurants. ₅₅ It's an excellent example of a BtoB company selling to other enterprises.

Notes

● l. 2：multihued 複数の色のついた、様々な● l. 2：whet someone's appetite （人の）興味をそそる● l. 3： flavor 味、風味● l. 4：appearance 見た目● l. 12：the 1920s 1920年代● l. 12：Shirokiya 白木屋：現在の 東急百貨店や阪急百貨店梅田店の前身となる老舗デパート● l. 13：predecessor 前身● l. 16：wax 蝋● l. 17： replica レプリカ、複製品● l. 25：hold a candle to ～に匹敵する● l. 27：Sogo そごう百貨店● l. 30： beneficiary 恩恵を受けたもの● l. 31：synthetic resin 合成樹脂● l. 32：elaborate 精巧な● l. 34：from scratch 最初（ゼロ）から● l. 37：picture-perfect （見た目が）完璧な● ll. 39-40：to the letter 厳密に ● l. 42：deter 思いとどませる● ll. 49-50：direct marketing item ダイレクトマーケティング商品：小売店など の中間業者を介さずに直接、消費者に製品を販売する方法● ll. 50-51：in-store fixture 店内什器（じゅうき） ● l. 56：BtoB 商取引の形態の一つ：企業と企業との間で取り交わされる取引のこと。Bはbusinessの意味。

2 ▶▶▶ Comprehension Questions

After reading the passage, choose either True (T), False (F), or "No information available in the passage"(?) for the statements below.

1. Japan started serving Western and Chinese dishes at restaurants before World War II. ( )

2. The first displayed sample was invented in around the 1920s. ( )

3. It was Mr. Iwasaki's wife who helped him to develop the best method for producing the food samples. ( )

4. Iwasaki offers online shopping for the food samples. ( )

5. Nowadays, Iwasaki is an essential partner for restaurants. ( )

3 ▶▶▶ One More Episode

🔊 Audio 2-06

Listen and fill in the blanks.

In 2011, Iwasaki opened Ganso Shokuhin Sample-ya, a place where regular people (1) _____ experience the amazing wonders of realistic food samples. There, visitors can buy painstakingly crafted replicas, food sample souvenirs (2) _____ as key rings, magnets, and straps, or (3) _____ a kit *Sample'n* to make their own models at home. (4) _____, a hands-on workshop teaches people about the production process. The facility is popular (5) _____ families and couples, as well as inbound tourists who excitedly snap photos of the realistic models. Ganso Shokuhin Sample-ya is a wonderland (6) ____ learning all about Japan's culture of enticing food presentation.

● **painstakingly** 苦労して ● **inbound tourists** 外国からくる旅行客 ● **enticing** 魅力的な

Step 4 ▶▶▶ Interaction

Make pairs and ask each other questions given below.

1. When you go to restaurants, do you look at the food samples to help you choose your order? Why?
2. Have you ever made a handcrafted thing (handmade wind chimes, photo album, etc.)? Why?

Step 5 ▶▶▶ Summary & Presentation

Q 1. Summarize the passage by using the following keywords.

food samples   department store   replica   founded

scratch   BtoB   satisfy   customers

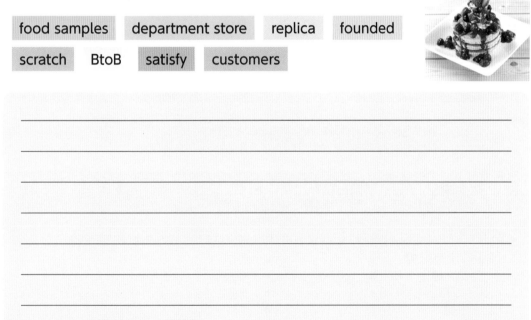

Q 2. **Make a presentation** of the summary made above.

Lesson 12

Kamoi Kakoshi
── Small tapes fascinate the world

海外から輸入された商品を実験と研究を重ね高品質な商品にパワーアップさせて売るという独自の方法を採ってきた同社の「mt」はいかに誕生したのだろうか。

Vocabulary Buildup

Match the words and phrases below with the correct meanings in Japanese.

1. spread across **2** ● ● 引き出す
2. explosive **2** ● ● 衛生的な
3. hygienic **3** ● ● 可能性のある
4. expand **3** ● ● 認められる
5. orchestrate **4** ● ● 偶然の一致
6. numerous **4** ● ● 組織化する、編成する
7. note **5** ● ● 多数の
8. potential **5** ● ● ～に散在する、広がる
9. independently **5** ● ● 独立して、自主的に
10. granted **5** ● ● それによって
11. overjoy **5** ● ● 大喜びする
12. thereby **5** ● ● 爆発的な
13. elicit **6** ● ● 着目する、留意する
14. coverage **6** ● ● 報道、取材
15. coincidence **8** ● ● 拡大する

Reading

🔊 Audio 2-07

1 Do you know the story of masking tape?

2 Originally an adhesive tape for keeping surfaces clean while painting, its intended purpose was for "masking," or covering. Masking tape first spread across Japan with the 1938 release of a variety made from *washi* paper, then became an explosive hit product in 2007. The driver of this boom was Kamoi Kakoshi Co., Ltd., a company in Okayama that created a product with a simple name: *mt*. 5

カモ井のハイトリ紙

3 When Kamoi Toshiro founded the enterprise in 1923, he sold the public a fly 10 trap to make living environments more hygienic. He had originally worked at a major bank, but his natural inventiveness had driven him to perform extensive experiments and research to develop a quality, affordable version of expensive imported fly traps. That year, the terrible sanitary conditions created by the Great Kanto 15 Earthquake was a boon that sent sales skyrocketing, while the company expanded into overseas markets.

創業者 鴨井利郎氏

4 In the difficult circumstances following World War II, Kamoi Kakoshi orchestrated a comeback with new products such as insecticide, and in 1961 entered a new 20 business: adhesive tape. By sending salespeople to visit the customers who used the product and taking their concerns seriously, the firm created numerous high-quality tapes. At last it grew into one 25 of the biggest players in the industrial masking tape sector.

5 Masking tape's use in arts and crafts began in 2006 when three women met up: a Tokyo café owner, her friend, and a graphic designer. Noting 30 the potential to use industrial masking tape as a decoration, they independently produced and distributed a book about tape. When making a follow-up, the women e-mailed Kamoi Kakoshi requesting a factory tour. It was granted and they were overjoyed. They then suggested a new tape product. At

3人の女性が制作したマスキングテープが主役の
リトルプレス *Masking Tape Guide Book*

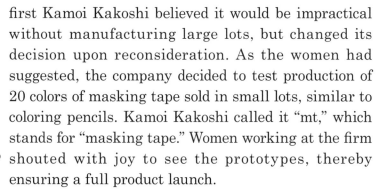

first Kamoi Kakoshi believed it would be impractical without manufacturing large lots, but changed its decision upon reconsideration. As the women had suggested, the company decided to test production of 20 colors of masking tape sold in small lots, similar to coloring pencils. Kamoi Kakoshi called it "mt," which stands for "masking tape." Women working at the firm shouted with joy to see the prototypes, thereby ensuring a full product launch.

6 Soon, *mt* became a big hit, especially among enthusiasts of stationery and knick-knacks. It won a Good Design Award in 2008 and elicited a strong response at the 2009 Maison&Objet trade fair in Paris. Heavy media coverage outside Japan followed thereafter, catapulting *mt* onto the global stage. The creativity and passion of *mt*'s three inventors drove a local adhesive tape maker to produce a new culture of cuteness around masking tape.

7 Kamoi Kakoshi employees hear from customers at events across Japan. They also have regularly scheduled planning meetings to make their ideas come true with *mt*'s designer sense. One unique thing is that to keep design consistent, the company largely relies on a single outside designer.

イベントの様子

This customer-first approach has always been part of the corporate culture.

8 With a consistent track record of manufacturing and selling excellent BtoB products while applying techniques to produce popular consumer goods, it's no coincidence that Kamoi Kakoshi doesn't just jump at opportunities, but rather has been addressing customer needs from the very beginning.

壁や床、ガラスにも貼れて楽しめる *mt casa* シリーズ

Notes

● l. 2：**adhesive** 粘着性の ● l. 3：**intended** 本来の、所期の ● l. 7：**driver**（活動に勢いを与える）けん引役 ● l. 10：**enterprise** 企業、事業 ● l. 14：**affordable** 手頃な価格の ● l. 14：**fly trap** ハエとり紙 ● l. 15：**sanitary condition** 衛生状態 ● ll. 15-16：**Great Kanto Earthquake** 関東大地震 ● l. 20：**insecticide** 殺虫剤 ● l. 27：**sector** 部門 ● ll. 28-29：**arts and crafts** 美術工芸 ● ll. 32-33：**making a follow-up** 〜の追跡調査を行う ● l. 35：**impractical** 実現困難な ● l. 42：**prototype** 試作品 ● l. 45：**knick-knacks** 小間物 ● l. 46：**Good Design Award** グッドデザイン賞：デザインが優れた物事に贈られる賞 ● l. 47：**Maison&Objet trade fair** メゾン・エ・オブジェ。フランス・パリで開催される世界最高峰のインテリアとデザイン関連見本市 ● l. 49：**catapult** 〜を勢いよく放り出す ● l. 58：**corporate culture** 社風

step 2 ▶▶▶ Comprehension Questions

After reading the passage, choose either True (T), False (F), or "No information available in the passage"(?) for the statements below.

1. Masking tape made from *washi* paper first spread across Japan in 1938. (　　)

2. It was not until after the Great Kanto Earthquake that masking tape was sold in the Kansai area.　　　　　　　　　　　　　　　　　　　　　　　(　　)

3. It was in 1961 when Kamoi Kakoshi started to produce masking tape.　(　　)

4. Kamoi Kakoshi consistently listens to the voices of consumers to maintain quality.　　　　　　　　　　　　　　　　　　　　　　　　　　　(　　)

5. The only purpose for masking tape is to cover a painting.　　　　(　　)

step 3 ▶▶▶ One More Episode

🔊 **Audio 2-08**

Listen and fill in the blanks.

Since 2012, Kamoi Kakoshi has held *mt factory tours* for a ⁽¹⁾_____ of two weeks every year. The ⁽²⁾_____ popular event attracts hordes of masking tape fans from across Japan to see how the product is produced. ⁽³⁾___ addition, during the tours, visitors can purchase limited-edition masking tape. There are ⁽⁴⁾_____ special

カモ井加工紙 矢掛工場 (岡山県小田郡)

novelty goods on offer. Recently, the company has instituted a lottery system ⁽⁵⁾_____ to the tours' overwhelming popularity. Lucky winners get to immerse themselves in the amazing world ⁽⁶⁾___ masking tape. If you get the opportunity to join, make the most of it!

● **hordes of** 多数の～ ● **lottery system** 抽選制度 ● **make the most of** ～を最大限に利用する

step 4 ▶▶▶ Interaction

Make pairs and ask each other questions given below.

1. When you write e-mails or send text-messages to your friends, do you decorate them with pictures, photos, etc.? Why?
2. Have you ever used a "customer voice" questionnaire? Why?

step 5 ▶▶▶ Summary & Presentation

Q 1. Summarize the passage by using the following keywords.

develop   fly trap   quality   new business

adhesive   masking tape   customer-first   maintain

_____
_____
_____
_____
_____
_____
_____

Q 2. **Make a presentation** of the summary made above.

Lesson 13 SEKISUI CHEMICAL 1 SEKISUI
—Perfect preparation and energy

INTRODUCTION 太陽光発電、環境重視の面で業界トップの実績を誇る同社の住宅。災害に強く、「安心と安全」を
モットーにした新商品開発のプロセスとは？

 1 ▶▶▶ Vocabulary Buildup

Match the words and phrases below with the correct meanings in Japanese.

1.	led ~ to **2**	● ● 積極的な
2.	coupled with **3**	● ● 促進する
3.	make full use of **3**	● ● 改良
4.	aggressive **3**	● ● 洗練された
5.	further **3**	● ● 相談、話し合い
6.	evolution **3**	● ● 進化
7.	sophisticated **3**	● ● 居住者
8.	distinguish **4**	● ● ～を十分に活用して
9.	assemble **4**	● ● ～から守る
10.	protect from **4**	● ● 安心感
11.	consultation **4**	● ● 組み立てられる
12.	emphasis on **5**	● ● ～に重点を置く
13.	residents **5**	● ● 区別する
14.	reassurance **5**	● ● ～と統合して
15.	undergo **6**	● ● ～を受ける
16.	refinement **7**	● ● ～につながった：lead の過去形

Reading

Audio 2-09

最初の自社工場となった奈良工場

ポリペールは日本のごみ収集システムを変えた

▲積水化学の最長寿製品の一つ
「セロハンテープ」

◀花嫁さんの支度品にもなっていた「ポリバケツ」

1 Sekisui Chemical Co., Ltd. was founded in 1947 as plastics manufacturer Sekisui Inc. The company took orders for ballpoint pens in postwar Japan, followed by cellophane tape, rain gutters, Poly-Pail garbage containers, pipes, and other plastic household goods. Due to massive growth into more businesses, in 2001, Sekisui Chemical organized itself into three divisional Companies. Sekisui Heim, the Housing Company, accounts for nearly half of sales.

2 Soaring housing demand during Japan's rapid growth led Sekisui Chemical to enter the housing business. After a successful trial in 1960, the housing business unit was split off as Sekisui House Industry, which remains an independent company now called Sekisui House.

3 During that time, the company began developing a novel approach to housing development with new construction methods based on knowledge about efficient production of quality plastic materials, coupled with the idea of making full use of plastic's advantages. In 1971,

セキスイハイム M1

Sekisui Heim released its first product: *SEKISUI HEIM M1*, followed by the 1982 launch of the *SEKISUI TWO-U HOME* constructed from wooden two-by-fours. These were among Sekisui Heim's aggressive innovations that furthered its evolution into a sophisticated housing company.

4 What distinguishes Sekisui Heim most is that it builds rooms and modules on a factory production line. These components are assembled on-site according to the company's groundbreaking "unit construction method."

建築現場へ移送された
ユニットを緊結設置

工場の生産ラインで家を構成する部屋やその一部である「ユニット」を製造するユニット工法

As this approach protects construction materials from rain, the entire home possesses high quality and durability. Furthermore, assembly only takes a day. Just a month later, interior decorations are finished, making for astounding cost performance. This method originated with the research and ideas of architect Ohno Katsuhiko, and now includes steel and wood module frames. Although modules are mass-produced, they offer great freedom for homebuyers in choosing exteriors and layouts in consultation with a planner.

5 In recent years, these homes have made the company the clear industry leader thanks to the installation of solar panels and an emphasis on green housing. The array of designs has recently grown from solar-powered homes that save on bills to the *Smart Heim* equipped with a storage battery and potable water retention, zero-power homes where residents can ride out a power outage, as well as resilient homes designed for a quick return to everyday life in a disaster's aftermath. In disaster-prone Japan, no other housing solution has enjoyed such success by prioritizing reassurance and safety.

スマートハイム

6 Extensive research is the basis for Sekisui Heim's product development. Resident surveys come in three varieties. The first involves quarterly meetings where regional sales company managers and development personnel from the head office meet customers to directly elicit their views. This way, the company can immediately gauge needs and areas for improvement. The second survey is a questionnaire periodically given to all resident

蓄電池設置例

households that inquires into satisfaction and needs. The results then undergo exhaustive analysis. Thirdly, company employees visit residents at home. This provides the most real-world understanding of how residents live, what makes them happy, and the issues they face. Sekisui Heim also has laboratories to

75 study lifestyles and housing technology. Lab workers research future consumer needs, untapped demand, and the latest technology. They also collaborate with the head office on product planning.

7 True to the Sekisui name, the company is creating the ideal home by leveraging all its strength toward years-long technological refinement,
80 exploration of customer needs, and comprehensive preparations. Sekisui Heim has an incredibly bright future.

Notes

● l. 3 : ballpoint pens ボールペン ● l. 4 : postwar 戦後の ● l. 4 : cellophane tape セロハンテープ ● l. 5 : rain gutters 雨樋。屋根などの雨水を受けて流す細長い樋 ● l. 5 : Poly-Pail ポリペール (商品名)：ゴミ箱などに使用される蓋つきのプラスチック容器。 ● l. 5 : garbage containers ゴミ箱 ● l. 11 : soaring 急上昇する ● l. 14 : business unit 部署 ● ll. 14-15 : split off 分社化 ● l. 27 : two-by-fours ツーバイフォー工法 ● l. 32 : production line 製造ライン ● l. 33 : on-site 現場で、現地で ● l. 34 : groundbreaking 革新的な、パイオニア的な ● l. 34 : unit construction method ユニット工法 ● l. 39 : assembly 組み立て ● l. 52 : installation 取り付け ● l. 52 : solar panel 太陽電池パネル、ソーラーパネル ● l. 53 : green housing グリーン住宅：環境に優しい家造りのこと ● l. 55 : save on bills 料金を節約する ● l. 56 : storage battery 家庭用蓄電池 ● l. 56 : potable 飲用に適した ● l. 56 : water retention 家庭用貯水槽 ● l. 57 : ride out ～を乗り越える ● l. 58 : power outage 停電 ● l. 58 : resilient 復元力のある ● l. 60 : aftermath (災害などの) 直後 ● l. 60 : disaster-prone 災害の多い ● l. 62 : reassurance 安心 ● l. 65 : quarterly meetings 四半期会議：年に4回行う会議 ● l. 66 : regional 地方の ● l. 67 : personnel 社員 ● l. 67 : head office 本社 ● l. 69 : gauge 判断する ● l. 70 : periodically 定期的に ● l. 76 : untapped 未開発の ● l. 78 : true to ... ～に忠実である、～に恥じぬように ● l. 79 : leveraging 活用する ● l. 79 : years-long 何年もの

step 2 ▸▸▸ Comprehension Questions

After reading the passage, choose either True (T), False (F), or "No information available in the passage"(?) for the statements below.

1. Sekisui Chemical Co., Ltd. started by selling stationery and other plastic household goods. ( )

2. The company started the housing business 2 years after the war. ( )

3. During the 1950s, Sekisui Chemical went through a period of trial and error to enter the housing business. ( )

4. The company holds a meeting every three months to check on the satisfaction of residents. ( )

5. The company is creating the ideal home by only using technology they have used previously. ( )

step 3 ▸▸▸ One More Episode

🔊 Audio 2-10

Listen and fill in the blanks.

Sekisui Heim's latest venture is urban development. *Asaka Leadtown* in Asaka, Saitama Prefecture is based on the concept ⁽¹⁾ ____ a "safe & sound, environmentally-friendly, sustainable town." The company is directing development projects ⁽²⁾ _____ include detached houses,

あさかリードタウン（埼玉県朝霞市）

apartment buildings, parks, and shopping centers. ⁽³⁾ ___ addition to detached houses, the town will have some ⁽⁴⁾ _____ products and services offered by the Sekisui Chemical Group, ⁽⁵⁾ _____ as construction materials, piping, rainwater storage materials, and other anti-disaster equipment, as well ⁽⁶⁾ ___ town management services.

● **sustainable** 持続可能な ● **detached house** 一戸建て住宅 ● **anti-disaster** 防災

step 4 ▶▶▶ Interaction

Make pairs and ask each other questions given below.

1. If you had the chance to build a house, what would your ideal house look like?
2. What is the thing that makes you happy in your daily life? Why?

step 5 ▶▶▶ Summary & Presentation

Q 1. Summarize the passage by using the following keywords.

split off   housing demand   construction   method

solar panel   disaster   survey   customer

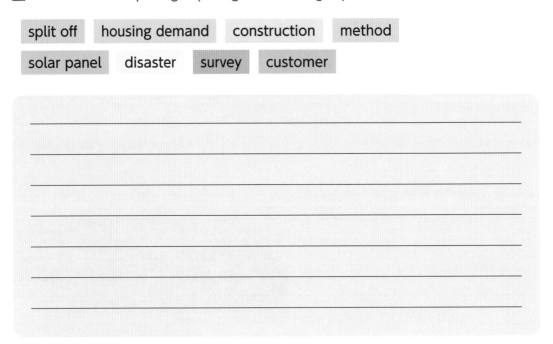

Q 2. Make a presentation of the summary made above.

14

SEKISUI CHEMICAL 2 SEKISUI

— Epoch-making product development in "BtoB"

INTRODUCTION 下水道管を更生する工法として、日本発の技術で世界で初めて特許を得た同社の SPR (Sewage Pipe Renewal) 工法。その画期的方法とは？

Step 1 ▶▶▶ Vocabulary Buildup

Match the words and phrases below with the correct meanings in Japanese.

1.	latter **1**	●	● 実行可能な
2.	parts **1**	●	● 主要な
3.	leading **2**	●	● 後者
4.	notable **3**	●	● 突破口
5.	collapse **3**	●	● ～を発展させる
6.	considerable **3**	●	● 注目に値する
7.	supplier **3**	●	● さもなければ
8.	breakthrough **3**	●	● 供給元、サプライヤー
9.	eliminate **3**	●	● 古くなる、劣化する
10.	mold **4**	●	● ～を伴う
11.	feasible **4**	●	● 相当な
12.	diverse **4**	●	● 崩壊する
13.	age **4**	●	● 取り組む
14.	accompany **4**	●	● 取り除く
15.	compatible **5**	●	● 相性がいい
16.	otherwise **5**	●	● 多様な
17.	tackle **6**	●	● 部品
18.	foster **6**	●	● 金型、鋳型

Lesson 14

Reading

🔊 Audio 2-11

私たちの生活を支えている積水化学の商品。左上から時計周りにユニットバス、空調配管、まくらぎ、航空機内装材

1 Sekisui Chemical comprises three divisional Companies. The Housing Company is a BtoC enterprise, while the Urban Infrastructure & Environmental Products Company (UIEP) and the High Performance Plastics Company are BtoB. The latter handles a wide range of plastic materials and parts, while UIEP's focus is on lifelines, manufacturing pipes for water, sewerage, and gas, which make modern living possible.

強化プラスチック複合管（エスロン RCP）

5

2 In 1952, five years after Sekisui Chemical's founding, the company began producing *Eslon pipes* (PVC pipes). More lightweight, resistant to corrosion, long-lasting, and reliable than conventional pipes, they came into use everywhere.

エスロンパイプ

水道配水用ポリエチレン管埋設工事の様子

10

3 One notable recent UIEP

15 innovation is the groundbreaking *SPR method* (*Sewage Pipe Renewal method*) for rehabilitating sewer pipes. Thirty years after sewer pipes were laid in urbanizing areas during Japan's rapid postwar growth, they began to age. When a pipe broke and the surrounding soil seeped inside, it created a hollow cavity in the ground. This was

20 the cause of many road collapses. Replacing the pipes incurred considerable time and expense to block them and dig up roads. As a major pipe supplier, UIEP joined a research project for Tokyo's government in 1986 that arrived at a unique solution: Old sewer pipes could be rehabilitated by winding spiraling strips of PVC resin inside of them. Applying this breakthrough by feeding the resin

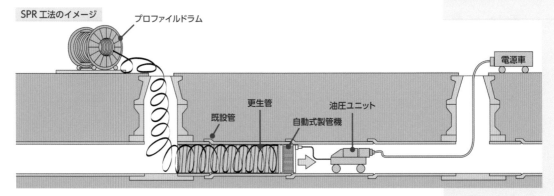

SPR 工法のイメージ　プロファイルドラム　電源車　既設管　更生管　油圧ユニット　自動式製管機

through a manhole eliminated the need to dig up roads or block sewer pipes. The material is also strong and earthquake-resistant. *SPR*'s success attracted customers in cities around the world. There are many methods for rehabilitating sewer pipes, but the *SPR* method from Japan was the first to be patented.

老朽化した下水道管を更生する SPR 工法

4 An Australian company's technology provided the hint for the spiral technique, which was used to make molds for cylindrical concrete shapes such as utility poles. UIEP studied its potential application for the entirely different purpose of rehabilitating sewer pipes and came up with *SPR*. It took 10 years to make it feasible for the diverse range of aging sewer pipes and worksite conditions. A major factor behind the success was that joint research with the Tokyo Bureau of Sewerage provided insights into sewer pipe needs. Many of the company's salespeople have engineering backgrounds or are accompanied by engineers to advise on construction methods and potential solutions.

5 The latest version, *SPR-SE*, is compatible with severely aged sewer pipes that are otherwise difficult to repair. While *SPR* strengthened old sewers by combining them with rehabilitated pipes, *SPR-SE* only employs resin to strengthen, a solution that overjoyed municipalities fretting about rehabilitating weak old pipes.

SPR-SE 工法による施工の様子

6 UIEP has always tackled vexing problems with infrastructure in society and our environment. When there is no precedent, a pioneer must find a way. This experience fostered the company's ambitions to develop innovative solutions by coordinating closely with municipalities, identifying unique local needs, proposing suitable methods, and performing the work. This approach allows the company to develop more sophisticated technology that leads to new solutions satisfying market needs. UIEP's management was patient during the 10 years of *SPR*'s development because they knew it would become a great innovation. This pioneer spirit, market insight, and advanced technology represent the ideal BtoB enterprise.

Notes

● l. 2 : **Infrastructure** 電気・ガス・水道・鉄道・道路など、生活の基礎となる設備 ● l. 6 : **sewerage** 下水道設備 ● l. 9 : *Eslon pipes* (PVC pipes) エスロンは商品名で、PVC（ポリ塩化ビニル）は polyvinyl chloride の略 ● l. 10 : **corrosion** 腐食 ● l. 11 : **conventional** 従来型の ● l. 16 : **rehabilitate** 元の状態に戻す ● l. 20 : **incurred** 生じた ● l. 23 : **spiraling** 螺旋状の ● l. 24 : **resin** 樹脂 ● l. 29 : **patent** 〜の特許権をとる ● l. 32 : **cylindrical** シリンダー（円柱・円筒）形の ● l. 33 : **utility pole** 電柱 ● ll. 37-38 : **Tokyo Bureau of Sewerage** 東京都下水道局 ● l. 46 : **fret about** 思い悩む ● l. 48 : **vexing problem** 厄介な問題 ● l. 49 : **precedent** 前例

step 2 ▶▶▶ Comprehension Questions

After reading the passage, choose either True (T), False (F), or "No information available in the passage"(?) for the statements below.

1. Sekisui Chemical Co., Ltd. focuses mainly on BtoC. ( )

2. Eslon is the name of the engineer who invented the PVC pipes. ( )

3. Changing the sewer pipes to new type needs vast money and time. ( )

4. It took more than a decade to come up with the spiral technique. ( )

5. The company is ambitious to develop innovative solutions for the local needs.

( )

step 3 ▶▶▶ One More Episode

🔊 Audio 2-12

Listen and fill in the blanks.

The company name Sekisui is a reference from "The Art of War," the treatise (1) _____ the ancient Chinese military strategist Sun Tsu that discusses "the importance of charging into battle in an onrush (2) _____ is like the bursting of pent-up waters (*sekisui* in Japanese) (3) _____ a chasm a thousand

積水化学が本店としていたこの大阪ビルヂングは当時大阪を代表するビルだった

fathoms deep." In other words, the (4) _____ Sekisui represents the company's approach to business: fighting to win with the force of a deluge of unleashed waters, but (5) _____ after thorough analysis, research, and preparation.

● "The Art of War" 『孫子の兵法』● treatise 専門書 ● Sun Tsu 孫武 (孫子) ● pent-up せき止めた ● fathom 尋 (ひろ)：水深の測定単位 ● in an onrush 一気に ● chasm 裂け目 ● deluge 大洪水

Step 4 ▶▶▶ Interaction

Make pairs and ask each other questions given below.

1. What is the thing you use daily that is made of plastic? Why?
2. What skills do you think a pioneer should have? Why?

Step 5 ▶▶▶ Summary & Presentation

Q 1. Summarize the passage by using the following keywords.

BtoB   lifeline   innovation   pipe

earthquake-resistant   patented   vexing   technology

_____

_____

_____

_____

_____

_____

_____

Q 2. **Make a presentation** of the summary made above.

15

How to Create 20 Ideas in 30 Minutes

INTRODUCTION アイデアを一から考えるということはなかなか難しいもの。本書の監修者・著者、神田範明氏の提唱する、ちょっとした工夫で今からでも実践できてしまう素晴らしい方法とは？

Step 1 ▶▶▶ Vocabulary Buildup

Match the words and phrases below with the correct meanings in Japanese.

1.	soar **1**	●	● 刺激する
2.	divine **2**	●	● 中間の
3.	no way with ... **2**	●	● 不快な
4.	stimulate **3**	●	● メモする
5.	disagreeable **3**	●	● 神の
6.	convenient **4**	●	● 特定する
7.	utensil **4**	●	● 上昇する
8.	jot down **5**	●	● ～はありえない
9.	trait **5**	●	● ばかげた
10.	intermediate **5**	●	● 便利な
11.	ridiculous **5**	●	● 特徴
12.	identify **6**	●	● 用具

Reading

🔊 Audio 2-13

1 Generating ideas is an essential business skill. When the boss asks for ideas during a planning meeting, you raise your hand and say, "I just came up with 20 I'd like to share. I thought of 5 them just 30 minutes ago, so many might not be good." After hearing your ideas, everyone is amazed because many *are* good. They wonder, "What an idea man. Did he really only take 30 minutes?" Your reputation soars. 10

2 Many people can't come up with ideas so well, but if you can share 20 ideas from half an hour before a meeting, others may think you have divine powers. This is something you can actually do. Why do we get stuck for ideas? Many times, the issue is psychological or has to do with our approach, but in either case you can address it. The psychological issue could be a negative attitude: 15 "Why can't I think of anything?"; "No way with our technology."; "We've failed so many times before." You close yourself off with narrow thinking. The brain cannot perform well in a negative condition. Simply breaking out of this situation requires considerable change. "It's better than doing nothing." "Stop being so serious." These kinds of feelings are important, and a boss must also 20 create this atmosphere. Criticism should come afterward.

3 The most important thing is your approach. Developing an idea means stimulating the brain (particularly the right side) to encourage novel thoughts. If that stimulus is fresh and pleasant, the brain is happy and begins working. Motivate the brain and avoid making it feel disagreeable or bothered. 25

4 To do this, we can apply *the Focusing Method* developed by Kanda Noriaki. Let's start with a simple example. You will now think of an idea for a new pen. Normally you might think about what makes a pen convenient, write smoothly, or look good. But this thinking won't lead to very inventive ideas. With this method, we first focus on the following: 30

   1. Something entirely or mostly unrelated to a pen or writing utensils
   2. Something you like 35

5 Let's say it's theme parks. Next, focus on theme parks and jot down all the words that come to mind. If you like theme parks, they should come easily.

tickets , cartoon characters , parades ...

The words should have little to do with pens or with each other. Write down what kinds of words these are and their traits, even if you can only think of one. These are the "intermediate ideas."

tickets → limited, pretty printing, anticipation of using

cartoon characters → happy to meet, cute merchandise

parades → anything can appear, splendid, set start time

And so forth. Next, connect one of these impressions with pens, even if the connection seems ridiculous.

tickets → limited → a pen that changes appearance over time

cartoon characters → happy to meet → a "lucky winner" pen

parades → anything can appear → a pen that writes in multiple colors

Now, type these out in an Excel spreadsheet.

6 Normally, it takes about an hour to enter 20 words from your subject of focus and complete an idea for each. With practice you can do it in 30 to 40 minutes. You can further speed up the process by identifying your favorite topics and writing them in a notebook.

A	B	C	D
		焦点発想法の例	
焦点を当てる対象＝カメラ			発想する商品＝レストラン
	要素	中間アイデア	商品アイデア
1	ズーム	拡大縮小	多人数の時にテーブルが拡大できる
2	スマホ	通信できる	メニューを押すだけで注文完了
3	シャッター	固定する	迷う時、質問に答えていくとその時の気分に合った料理を教えてくれる
4	逆光	反対側	厨房での料理の進行状況がスマホで見られる
5	海の風景	海や山のイメージ	海、山、川、畑などにちなんだ日替わりメニューがいくつか並ぶ
6	コントラスト	幅がある	どの料理も味が薄い～濃い、甘い～辛い量が少ない～多いなどが指定できる
7	アルバム	思い出	前回までの注文メニューを記録してあり、好みに合った料理を勧めてくれる
8	色彩	美しい	絵画のようにきれいな料理のレストラン
9	瞬間	1/100秒	「他店の100倍美味しい」レストラン
10	LINE	スタンプ	毎回楽しいサプライズのプレゼントがある

7 When you try *the Focusing Method* for yourself, you'll see how original thoughts gush forth. That's because you're thinking from an entirely different perspective from usual. You'll come up with numerous fresh yet useful ideas.

8 Changing your point of view is the key to making *the Focusing Method* intuitive and simple.

 **Notes**

● l. 17 : close yourself off ～から離れて ● l. 26 : *the Focusing Method* 焦点発想法 ● l. 47 : anticipation of using 使用への期待感 ● l. 68 : gush forth 湧き出る ● l. 72 : intuitive 直感で理解できる

step 2 ▶▶▶ Comprehension Questions

After reading the passage, choose either True (T), False (F), or "No information available in the passage"(?) for the statements below.

1. If you have many good ideas to share, it is better for you to jot them down on a notebook. ( )

2. If your ideas are good, your reputation will grow. ( )

3. It is better to start thinking from a simple example. ( )

4. Every theme park has a parade which entertains guests. ( )

5. If you practice for a day, it is easy to come up with 20 ideas in 30 minutes.
( )

step 3 ▶▶▶ One More Episode

📶 **Audio 2-14**

Listen and fill in the blanks.

"Your idea sounds good, but tell me why."
"Why don't you understand why it's so great?!"
The brain works differently (1) ___ different people. For some, the logical left brain and the emotional right brain work in sync, (2) _____ in others, the hemispheres have a weak connection. Women (3) _____ to be the former, while men are often the latter. It would seem that the structure (4) ___ the brain is not unrelated to a preference for communication employing the entire brain, or a preference (5) ____ deeply exploring a hobby or other subject matter on one's own.

● **work in sync** 同時に働く ● **hemisphere** 脳の半球 ● **preference** 好み ● **explore** ～を探索する

ˢᵗᵉᵖ 4 ▶▶▶ Interaction

Make pairs and ask each other questions given below.

> 1. Can you come up with an idea for a new product (e.g. smartphone)? Explain your idea.
> 2. How do you motivate yourself to study?

ˢᵗᵉᵖ 5 ▶▶▶ Summary & Presentation

Q 1. Summarize the passage by using the following keywords.

business   idea   reputation   *The Focusing Method*

jot down   connect   practice   useful

Q 2. **Make a presentation** of the summary made above.

||| 監修／著者・編著者・訳者紹介 |||

神田範明（かんだ　のりあき）

成城大学名誉教授。経営学（マーケティング）の研究者。専門は商品企画、市場調査、統計解析。

1949 年生まれ。東京工業大学工学部経営工学科、同大学院博士課程を経て名古屋商科大学商学部助教授、教授。1993 年より成城大学経済学部経営学科教授（同大学院教授を兼務）し、2020 年退職。この間、システマティックな商品企画の手法を世界で初めて体系化した「商品企画七つ道具」を発表（1994 年）、企業約 110 社と産学協同研究を行ない、日産自動車 X-TRAIL、アサヒ飲料 WONDA モーニングショットなどから飲食品、化粧品、住宅、自動車、電気、生活・娯楽、サービス、BtoB まで広範囲の業種で多数の商品企画を指導した。著書に『ものづくり教科書・革新のための 7 つの手法』（日経 BP 社）、『商品企画七つ道具実践シリーズ 第 1 巻「はやわかり編」、第 2 巻「よくわかる編」、第 3 巻「すぐできる編」』（編著、日科技連出版社）、「神田教授の商品企画ゼミナール」（単著、日科技連出版社）など多数。

2012 年から一般社団法人・日本マーケティング・リテラシー協会会長、2020 年から同会 WAKU WAKU 創造 LABO（略称 WAKU LABO）のチーフ・アドバイザーとして学生（すべて無料）、企業人対象の講演会、セミナー、産学協同商品企画プロジェクトを推進。また、同会では教授の発案により 2012 年から「商品企画士」の資格を創設し、検定試験を実施している。　WAKU LABO 公式 HP ▶

新原由希恵（しんはら　ゆきえ）

関西大学大学院外国語教育学研究科博士課程前期課程、英国ウォーリック大学大学院（University of Warwick）修了。

竹内　理（たけうち　おさむ）

関西大学外国語学部教授。神戸市外国語大学卒業、神戸市外国語大学大学院外国語学研究科（英語学）修了。モントレー大学大学院（Monterey Institute of International Studies）修了（英語教育学）。専門は応用言語学、外国語教育学。著書に『より良い外国語学習法を求めて──外国語学習成功者の研究』（松柏社）、『「達人」の英語学習法──データが語る効果的な外国語習得法とは』（草思社）、共編著書に『外国語教育研究ハンドブック──研究手法のより良い理解のために』（松柏社）など多数。訳書にテランス・ディックス『とびきり陽気なヨーロッパ史』（尾崎寔監修、ちくま文庫）、ゾルタン・ドルニェイ『外国語教育学のための質問紙調査入門──作成・実施・データ処理』（共訳、松柏社）など。

アレクサンダー・ファレル（Alexander Farrell）

米国テキサス大学オースティン校歴史学科卒業、サルヴェ・レジーナ大学大学院国際関係学科修了。

2003 年より京都市在住。日英翻訳者として、日本政府観光局をはじめ、ノンフィクション作品・書籍、ニュース・雑誌記事、広告、企業プレスリリース等に数多く携わる。関西地方を中心に全国の観光地の旅行記事を作成し、トラベルライターとして現地取材も行なっているほか、Alamy、Getty Images でトラベルフォトグラファーとしても活動している。英語教科書に *America Today* 『米国の今：文化・社会・歴史』（松柏社）、*America's Evolution* 『今のアメリカ、これからのアメリカ』（松柏社）。　HP ▶

Creative Ideas for Products & Services
商品開発の現場から──アイデア・人・モノの融合

2021 年 4 月 5 日　初版第 1 刷発行
2023 年 4 月 5 日　初版第 2 刷発行

監修・著者　　神田範明
編著者　　　　新原由希恵／竹内　理
文　　　　　　アレクサンダー・ファレル

発行者　　　　森　信久
発行所　　　　株式会社　松柏社
　　　　　　　〒102-0072　東京都千代田区飯田橋 1-6-1
　　　　　　　TEL　03（3230）4813（代表）
　　　　　　　FAX　03（3230）4857
　　　　　　　http://www.shohakusha.com
　　　　　　　e-mail: info@shohakusha.com

装幀　　　　　小島トシノブ（NONdesign）
本文レイアウト　一柳　茂（株式会社クリエーターズユニオン）
組版　　　　　木野内宏行（ALIUS）
印刷・製本　　日経印刷株式会社

略号＝ 772
ISBN978-4-88198-772-8